Improve
Interpersonal Skills

ManageMentor Skill Pack

Lesson From,

Linda Hill, John Gabarro, David Baldwin, Bill George,
Peter Drucker, Nick Craig, David Rooke, Ronald Heifetz,
Michael Watkins, John P. Kotter

A CIP catalogue record for this title is available from the British
Library
ISBN: 1515052117

ISBN-13: 978-1515052111

Printed and bound by
Amazon Media EU S.à r.l. , 5 Rue Plaetis, L-2338 Luxemburg.

Amazon.com, Inc.; Seattle, WA 98108-1226, USA

CONTENTS

ACKNOWLEDGMENTS

- *Michael D. Watkins* is a cofounder of Genesis Advisers, a leadership development firm specializing in onboarding and transition acceleration, and a professor at IMD. He is the author of The First 90 Days and Your Next Move (both from Harvard Business Press).

- *Ronald A. Heifetz* is codirector of the Center for Public Leadership at Harvard University's John F. Kennedy School of Government in Cambridge, Massachusetts.

- *David Rooke* is a partner at Harthill Consulting in Hewelsfield, England. William R. Torbert is a professor at Boston College's Carroll School of Management in Massachusetts. They are coauthors of Action Inquiry: The Secret of Timely and Transforming Leadership (Berrett-Koehler, 2004).

- *Nick Craig* is the president of the Authentic Leadership Institute. Scott Snook is the MBA Class of 1958 Senior Lecturer of Business Administration at Harvard Business School.

- *Peter F. Drucker* is the Marie Rankin Clarke Professor of Social Science and Management at the Peter F. Drucker and Masatoshi Ito Graduate School of Management at Claremont Graduate University in Claremont, California. He has written nearly two dozen articles for HBR.

- *Bill George*, the former chairman and CEO of Medtronic, is a professor of management practice at Harvard Business School in Boston.

- *David G. Baldwin* was a relief pitcher for the Washington Senators (now the Texas Rangers),the Milwaukee Brewers,and the Chicago White Sox during the 1960s and early 1970s. He played for various managers and coaches,including the legendary Ted Williams.

- *Mr. Nichols*, who heads up a Communications Program at the University of Minnesota, is nationally known for his many articles and lectures on communication problems.

- *Mr. Stevens* is a free-lance writer and a consultant on oral presentation to a number of leading companies and also is affiliated with Management Development Associates of New York. For two years he served as News Editor and Newscaster for educational radio station WSUI in Iowa City.

- *John J. Gabarro* is the UPS Foundation Professor of Human Resource Management at Harvard Business School in Boston.

- Now retired, *John P. Kotter* was the Konosuke Matsushita Professor of Leadership at Harvard Business School.

- *Linda A. Hill* is the Wallace Brett Donham Professor of Business Administration at Harvard Business School. She is the coauthors of Being the Boss: The 3 Imperatives for Becoming a Great Leader (Harvard Business Review Press, 2011).

- *Jean-François* Manzoni is an associate professor of management at Insead in Fontainebleau, France, and the director of the Insead PricewaterhouseCoopers Research Initiative on High- Performance Organizations. He is a coauthor, along with Jean- Louis Barsoux, of *The Set-Upto-Fail Syndrome: How Good Managers Cause Great People to Fail* (Harvard Business School Press, 2002)

CHAPTER 1

Are You A Good Boss Or a Great One?

If you want to keep growing as a leader, ask yourself these key questions. *by Linda A. Hill and Kent Lineback*

"Am I good enough?" These thoughts plagued Jason, an experienced manager, as he lay awake one night fretting about a new position he'd taken. For more than five years he had run a small team of developers in Boston. They produced two highly successful lines of engineering textbooks for the education publishing arm of a major media conglomerate. On the strength of his reputation as a great manager of product development, he'd been chosen by the company to take over an online technical-education start-up based in London.

Jason arrived at his new office on a Monday morning, excited and confident, but by the end of his first week he was beginning to wonder whether he was up to the challenge. In his previous work he had led people who'd worked together before and required coordination but little supervision. There were problems, of course, but nothing like what he'd discovered in this new venture. Key members of his group barely talked to one another. Other publishers in the company, whose materials and collaboration he desperately needed, angrily viewed his new group as competition. The goals he'd been set seemed impossible—the group was about to miss some early milestones—and a crucial partnership with an outside organization had been badly, perhaps irretrievably, damaged. On top of all that, his boss, who was located in New York, offered little help. "That's why you're there" was the typical response whenever Jason described a problem. By Friday he was worried about living up to the expectations implied in that response.

"Am I ready? This is my big opportunity, but now I'm not sure I'm prepared." Do Jason's feelings sound familiar? Such moments of doubt and even fear may and often do come despite years of management experience. Any number of events can trigger them: An initiative you're running isn't going as expected. Your people aren't performing as they should. You hear talk in the group that "the real problem here is lack of leadership." You think you're doing fine until you, like Jason, receive a daunting new assignment. You're given a lukewarm performance review. Or one day you simply realize that you're no longer growing and advancing—you're stuck.

Most Managers Stop Working on Themselves

The whole question of how managers grow and advance is one we've studied, thought about, and lived with for years. As a professor working with high potentials, MBAs, and executives from around the globe, Linda meets people who want to contribute to their organizations and build fulfilling careers. As an executive, Kent has worked with managers at all levels of both private and public organizations. All our experience brings us to a simple but troubling observation: Most bosses reach a certain level of proficiency and stop there—short of what they could and should be.

We've discussed this observation with countless colleagues, who almost without exception have seen what we see: Organizations usually have a few great managers, some capable ones, a horde of mediocre ones, some poor ones, and some awful ones. The great majority of people we work with are wellintentioned, smart, accomplished individuals. Many progress and fulfill their ambitions. But too many derail and fail to live up to their potential. Why? Because they stop working on themselves.

3

Managers rarely ask themselves, "How good am I?" and "Do I need to be better?" unless they're shocked into it. When did *you* last ask those questions? On the spectrum of great to awful bosses, where do you fall?

Managers in new assignments usually start out receptive to change. The more talented and ambitious ones choose stretch assignments, knowing that they'll have much to learn at first. But as they settle in and lose their fear of imminent failure, they often grow complacent. Every organization has its ways of doing things—policies, standard practices, and unspoken guidelines, such as "promote by seniority" and "avoid conflict." Once they're learned, managers often use them to get by—to "manage" in the worst sense of the word.

It doesn't help that a majority of the organizations we see offer their managers minimal support and rarely press the experienced ones to improve. Few expect more of their leaders than short-term results, which by themselves don't necessarily indicate real management skill.

In our experience, however, the real culprit is neither managerial complacency nor organizational failure: It is a lack of understanding. When bosses are questioned, it's clear that many of them have stopped making progress because they simply *don't know how to.*

Do you understand what's required to become truly effective? Too often managers underestimate how much time and effort it takes to keep growing and developing. Becoming a great boss is a lengthy, difficult process of learning and change, driven mostly by personal experience. Indeed, so much time and effort are required that you can think of the process as a journey—a journey of years.

What makes the journey especially arduous is that the lessons involved cannot be taught. Leadership is using yourself as an instrument to get things done in the organization, so it is about self-development. There are no secrets and few shortcuts. You and every other manager must learn the lessons yourself, based on your own experience as a boss. If you don't understand the nature of the journey, you're more likely to pause or lose hope and tell yourself, "I can't do this" or "I'm good enough already."

Do you understand what you're trying to attain? We all know how disorganized, fragmented, and even chaotic every manager's workdays are. Given this reality, which is intensifying as work and organizations become more complex and fluid, how can you as a boss do anything more than cope with what comes at you day by day?

To deal with the chaos, you need a clear underlying sense of what's important and where you and your group want to be in the future. You need a mental model that you can lay over the chaos and into which you can fit all the messy pieces as they come at you. This way of thinking begins with a straightforward definition: Management is responsibility for the performance of a group of people.

It's a simple idea, yet putting it into practice is difficult, because management is *defined* by responsibility but *done* by exerting influence. To influence others you must make a difference not only in what they do but also in the thoughts and feelings that drive their actions. How do you actually do this?

To answer that question, you need an overarching, integrated way of thinking about your work as a manager. We offer an approach based on studies of management practice, our own observations, and our knowledge of where managers tend to go wrong. We call it the *three imperatives:* Manage yourself. Manage your network. Manage your team.

Is this the only way to describe management? No, of course not. But it's clear, straightforward, and, above all, focused on what managers must actually do. People typically think of "management" as just the third imperative, but today all three are critical to success. Together they encompass the crucial activities that effective managers must perform to influence others. Mastering them is the purpose of your journey.

Manage Yourself

Management begins with you, because who you are as a person, what you think and feel, the beliefs and values that drive your actions, and especially how you connect with others all matter to the people you must influence. Every day those people examine every interaction with you, your every word and deed, to uncover your intentions. They ask themselves, "Can I trust this person?" How hard they work, their level of personal commitment, their willingness to accept your influence, will depend in large part on the qualities they see in you. And their perceptions will determine the answer to this fundamental question every manager must ask: Am I someone who can influence others productively?

Who you are shows up most clearly in the relationships you form with others, especially those for whom you're responsible. It's easy to get those crucial relationships wrong. Effective managers possess the self-awareness and self-management required to get them right.

José, a department head, told us of two managers who worked for him in the marketing department of a large maker of durable goods. Both managers were struggling to deliver the results expected of their groups. Both, it turned out, were creating dysfunctional relationships. One was frankly ambivalent about being "the boss" and hated it when people referred to him that way. He wanted to be liked, so he tried to build close personal relationships. He would say, in effect, "Do what I ask because we're friends." That worked for a while until, for good reasons, he had to turn down one "friend" for promotion and deny another one a bonus. Naturally, those people felt betrayed, and their dissatisfaction began to poison the feelings of everyone else in the group.

The other manager took the opposite approach. With her it was all business. No small talk or reaching out to people as people. For her, results mattered, and she'd been made the boss because she was the one who knew what needed to be done; it was the job of her people to execute. Not surprisingly, her message was always "Do what I say because I'm the boss." She was effective—until people began leaving.

If productive influence doesn't arise from being liked ("I'm your friend!") or from fear ("I'm the boss!"), where does it come from? From people's trust in you as a manager. That trust has two components: belief in your *competence* (you know what to do and how to do it) and belief in your *character* (your motives are good and you want your people to do well).

Trust is the foundation of all forms of influence other than coercion, and you need to conduct yourself with others in ways that foster it. Management really does begin with who you are as a person.

Manage Your Network

We once talked to Kim, the head of a software company division, just as he

was leaving a meeting of a task force consisting of his peers. He had proposed a new way of handling interdivisional sales, which he believed would increase revenue by encouraging each division to cross-sell other divisions' products. At the meeting he'd made an extremely well-researched, carefully reasoned, and even compelling case for his proposal—which the group rejected with very little discussion. "How many of these people did you talk to about your proposal before the meeting?" we asked. None, it turned out. "But I anticipated all their questions and objections," he protested, adding with some bitterness, "It's just politics. If they can't see what's good for the company and them, I can't help them."

Many managers resist the need to operate effectively in their organizations' political environments. They consider politics dysfunctional—a sign the organization is broken—and don't realize that it unavoidably arises from three features inherent in all organizations: *division of labor,* which creates disparate groups with disparate and even conflicting goals and priorities; *interdependence,* which means that none of those groups can do their work without the others; and *scarce resources,* for which groups necessarily compete. Obviously, some

5

organizations handle the politics better than others, but conflict and competition among groups are inevitable. How do they get resolved? Through organizational influence. Groups whose managers have influence tend to get what they need; other groups don't.

Unfortunately, many managers deal with conflict by trying to avoid it. "I hate company politics!" they say. "Just let me do my job." But effective managers know they cannot turn away. Instead, with integrity and for good ends, they proactively engage the organization to create the conditions for their success. They build and nurture a broad network of ongoing relationships with those they need and those who need them; that is how they influence people over whom they have no formal authority. They also take responsibility for making their boss, a key member of their network, a source of influence on their behalf.

Manage Your Team

As a manager, Wei worked closely with each of her people, who were spread across the U.S. and the Far East. But she rarely called a virtual group meeting, and only once had her group met face-to-face. "In my experience," she told us, "meetings online or in person are usually a waste of time. Some people do all the yakking, others stay silent, and not much gets done. It's a lot more efficient for me to work with each person and arrange for them to coordinate when that's necessary." It turned out, though, that she was spending all her time "coordinating," which included a great deal of conflict mediation. People under her seemed to be constantly at odds, vying for the scarce resources they needed to achieve their disparate goals and complaining about what others were or were not doing.

Too many managers overlook the possibilities of creating a real team and managing their people as a whole. They don't realize that managing one-on-one is just not the same as managing a group and that they can influence individual behavior much more effectively through the group, because most of us are social creatures who want to fit in and be accepted as part of the team. How do you make the people who work for you, whether on a project or permanently, into a real team—a group of people who are mutually committed to a common purpose and the goals related to that purpose?

To do collective work that requires varied skills, experience, and knowledge, teams are more creative and productive than groups of individuals who merely cooperate. In a real team, members hold themselves and one another jointly accountable. They share a genuine conviction that they will succeed or fail together. A clear and compelling purpose, and concrete goals and plans based on that purpose, are critical. Without them no group will coalesce into a real team.

Team culture is equally important. Members need to know what's required of them collectively and individually; what the team's values, norms, and standards are; how members are expected to work together (what kind of conflict is acceptable or unacceptable, for example); and how they should communicate. It's your job to make sure they have all this crucial knowledge.

Effective managers also know that even in a cohesive team they cannot ignore individual members. Every person wants to be a valued member of a group *and* needs individual recognition. You must be able to provide the attention members need, but always in the context of the team.

And finally, effective managers know how to lead a team through the work it does day after day—including the unplanned problems and opportunities that frequently arise—to make progress toward achieving their own and the team's goals.

Be Clear on How You're Doing

The three imperatives will help you influence both those who work for you and those who don't. Most important, they provide a clear and actionable road map for your journey. You must master them to become a fully effective manager.

These imperatives are not simply distinct managerial competencies. They are tightly integrated activities, each of which depends on the others. Getting your person-to-person relationships right is critical to building a well-functioning team and giving its individual members the attention they need. A compelling team purpose, bolstered by clear goals and plans, is the foundation for a strong network, and a network is indispensable for reaching your team's goals.

Knowing where you're going is only the first half of what's required. You also need to know at all times where you are on your journey and what you must do to make progress. We're all aware that the higher you rise in an organization, the less feedback you get about your performance. You have to be prepared to regularly assess yourself.

Too many managers seem to assume that development happens automatically. They have only a vague sense of the goal and of where they stand in relation to it. They tell themselves, "I'm doing all right" or "As I take on more challenges, I'll get better." Consequently, those managers fall short. There's no substitute for routinely taking a look at yourself and how you're doing. (The section "Measuring Yourself on the Three Imperatives" will help you do this.)

Don't be discouraged if you find several areas in which you could do better. No manager will meet all the standards implicit in the three imperatives. The goal is not perfection. It's developing the strengths you need for success and compensating for any fatal shortcomings. Look at your strengths and weaknesses in the context of your organization. What knowledge and skills does it—or will it—need to reach its goals? How can your strengths help it move forward? Given its needs and priorities, what weaknesses must you address right away? The answers become your personal learning goals.

Measuring Yourself on the Three Imperatives

How did you do? Did your responses cover the whole range from 1 to 5? If you consistently assessed yourself at 3 or above, you should be skeptical. In our experience, few bosses merit high ratings across the board. Did you give yourself mostly 3s? Take care not to hide in the middle, telling yourself, "I'm OK—not great, but not failing either." And don't be satisfied to stay there. "I'm not failing" is the watchword of those who are comfortable and stuck.

What You Can Do Right Now

Progress will come only from your work experience: from trying and learning, observing and interacting with others, experimenting, and sometimes pushing yourself beyond the bounds of comfort and then assessing yourself on the three imperatives again and again. Above all, take responsibility for your own development; ultimately, all development is selfdevelopment.

You won't make progress unless you consciously act. Before you started a business, you would draw up a business plan broken into manageable steps with milestones; do the same as you think about your journey. Set personal goals. Solicit feedback from others. Take advantage of company training programs. Create a network of trusted advisers, including role models and mentors. Use your strengths to seek out developmental experiences. We know you've heard all this advice before, and it is good advice. But what we find most effective is building the learning into your daily work.

For this purpose we offer a simple approach we call *prep, do, review*.

Prep. Begin each morning with a quick preview of the coming day's events. For each one, ask yourself how you can use it to develop as a manager and in particular how you can work on your specific learning goals. Consider delegating a task you would normally take on yourself and think about how you might do that—to whom, what questions you should ask, what boundaries or limits you should set, what preliminary coaching you might provide. Apply the same thinking during the day when a problem comes up unexpectedly. Before taking any action, step back and consider how it might help you become better. Stretch yourself. If you don't move outside familiar patterns and practice new approaches, you're unlikely to learn.

		I NEED TO MAKE PROGRESS				THIS IS A STRENGTH
1. Do you use your formal authority effectively?	THIS IS A STRENGTH IF you consider it a useful tool but not your primary means of influencing others. You make clear why you do what you do—and earn share your authority with others when possible and appropriate. You focus more on the responsibilities that come with authority than on the personal privileges it provides.	1	2	3	4	5
2. Do you create thoughtful but not overly personal relationships?	THIS IS A STRENGTH IF your relationships are rich in human connections but always focused on the purpose and goals of the team and the organization. You avoid trying to influence people by befriending them.	1	2	3	4	5
3. Do others trust you as a manager?	THIS IS A STRENGTH IF people, particularly your own, believe in your competence, intentions, and values. You demonstrate concern for their individual success.	1	2	3	4	5
4. Do you exercise your influence ethically?	THIS IS A STRENGTH IF you consistently identify stakeholders, weigh their interests, and try to mitigate any harm that your actions may cause as you attempt to accomplish a greater good.	1	2	3	4	5
5. Do you systematically identify those who should be in your network?	THIS IS A STRENGTH IF you are always aware of which people and groups you and your team depend on, and vice versa, as circumstances change.	1	2	3	4	5
6. Do you proactively build and maintain your network?	THIS IS A STRENGTH IF you create and sustain relationships with those in your network, connect frequently with them, and support their needs.	1	2	3	4	5
7. Do you use your network to provide the protection and resources your team needs?	THIS IS A STRENGTH IF you protect your team from distractions and misunderstandings, use your network to solve problems inside and outside the team, and secure the funds, people, and other resources it needs.	1	2	3	4	5
8. Do you use your network to accomplish your team's goals?	THIS IS A STRENGTH IF you form coalitions of network members to support your team's goals and help actors in your network achieve theirs. Your network colleagues believe in your competence and character.	1	2	3	4	5
9. Do you define and constantly refine your team's vision for the future?	THIS IS A STRENGTH IF you've defined your team's purpose and the goals, strategies, and actions that will take you there. You constantly gather information, discuss your plans with others, and refine your ideas.	1	2	3	4	5
10. Do you clarify roles, work rules, team culture, and feedback about performance for your team?	THIS IS A STRENGTH IF your people feel a strong sense of "we"—that they're all pulling together toward the same worthwhile goals. They know how they individually contribute and what the team's work involves. They receive regular feedback from you.	1	2	3	4	5
11. Do you know and manage your people as individuals as well as team members?	THIS IS A STRENGTH IF you interact equitably with all team members individually. You delegate, strive to help people grow, and constantly assess their performance. You hire people who both fit the team and add diversity, and you deal with performance issues quickly.	1	2	3	4	5
12. Do you use daily activities and problems to pursue the three imperatives?	THIS IS A STRENGTH IF you regularly consider how every problem, obligation, or event can help you build your team, make progress on its goals, develop people, and strengthen your network.	1	2	3	4	5

Do. Take whatever action is required in your daily work, and as you do, use the new and different approaches you planned. Don't lose your resolve. For example, if you tend to cut off conflict in a meeting, even constructive conflict, force yourself to hold back so that disagreement can be expressed and worked through. Step in only if the discussion becomes personal or points of view are being stifled. The ideas that emerge may lead you to a better outcome.

Review. After the action, examine what you did and how it turned out. This is where learning actually occurs. Reflection is critical, and it works best if you make it a regular practice. For example, set aside time toward the end of each day—perhaps on your commute home. Which actions worked well? What might you have done differently? Replay conversations. Compare what you did with what you might have done if you were the manager you aspire to be. Where did you disappoint yourself, and how did that happen? Did you practice any new behaviors or otherwise make progress on your journey?

Some managers keep notes about how they spent their time, along with thoughts about what they learned. One CEO working on a corporate globalization strategy told us he'd started recording every Friday his reflections about the past week. Within six weeks, he said, he'd developed greater discipline to say no to anything "not on the critical path," which gave him time to spend with key regulators and to jump-start the strategy.

If you still need to make progress on your journey, that should spur you to action, not discourage you. You can become what you want and need to be. But you must take personal responsibility for mastering the three imperatives and assessing where you are now.

The Idea in Brief

Many managers underestimate the transformational challenges of their roles—or they become complacent and stop growing and improving. At best they learn to get by; at worst they become terrible bosses. Sometimes even the best of them suffer doubts and fears despite years of management experience.

Three imperatives can guide managers on their journey to becoming great bosses: (1) *Manage yourself.* Productive influence comes from people's trust in your competence and character. (2) *Manage your network.* The organization as a whole must be engaged to create the conditions for your own and your team's success. (3) *Manage your team.* Effective managers forge a highperforming "we" out of all the individuals who report to them.

Constant and probing self-assessment across these three imperatives is essential, the authors write. They include a useful assessment tool to help readers get started.

CHAPTER 2

Crucibles Skills of Leadership

As lifelong students of leadership, we are fascinated with the notion of what makes a leader. Why is it that certain people seem to naturally inspire confidence, loyalty, and hard work, while others (who may have just as much vision and smarts) stumble, again and again? It's a timeless question, and there's no simple answer. But we have come to believe it has something to do with the different ways that people deal with adversity. Indeed, our recent research has led us to conclude that one of the most reliable indicators and predictors of true leadership is an individual's ability to find meaning in negative events and to learn from even the most trying circumstances. Put another way, the skills required to conquer adversity and emerge stronger and more committed than ever are the same ones that make for extraordinary leaders.

Take Sidney Harman. Thirty-four years ago, the then-48-year-old businessman was holding down two executive positions. He was the chief executive of Harman Kardon (now Harman International), the audio components company he had cofounded, and he was serving as president of Friends World College, now Friends World Program, an experimental Quaker school on Long Island whose essential philosophy is that students, not their teachers, are responsible for their education. Juggling the two jobs, Harman was living what he calls a "bifurcated life," changing clothes in his car and eating lunch as he drove between Harman Kardon offices and plants and the Friends World campus. One day while at the college, he was told his company's factory in Bolivar, Tennessee, was having a crisis.

He immediately rushed to the Bolivar factory, a facility that was, as Harman now recalls, "raw, ugly, and, in many ways, demeaning." The problem, he found, had erupted in the polish and buff department, where a crew of a dozen workers, mostly African-Americans, did the dull, hard work of polishing mirrors and other parts, often under unhealthy conditions. The men on the night shift were supposed to get a coffee break at 10 PM. When the buzzer that announced the workers' break went on the fritz, management arbitrarily decided to postpone the break for ten minutes, when another buzzer was scheduled to sound. But one worker, "an old black man with an almost biblical name, Noah B. Cross," had "an epiphany," as Harman describes it. "He said, literally, to his fellow workers, 'I don't work for no buzzer. The buzzer works for me. It's my job to tell me when it's ten o'clock. I got me a watch. I'm not waiting another ten minutes. I'm going on my coffee break.' And all 12 guys took their coffee break, and, of course, all hell broke loose."

The worker's principled rebellion—his refusal to be cowed by management's senseless rule—was, in turn, a revelation to Harman: "The technology is there to serve the men, not the reverse," he remembers realizing. "I suddenly had this awakening that everything I was doing at the college had appropriate applications in business." In the ensuing years, Harman revamped the factory and its workings, turning it into a kind of campus—offering classes on the premises, including piano lessons, and encouraging the workers to take most of the responsibility for running their workplace. Further, he created an environment where dissent was not only tolerated but also encouraged. The plant's lively independent newspaper, the Bolivar Mirror, gave workers a creative and emotional outlet—and they enthusiastically skewered Harman in its pages.

Harman had, unexpectedly, become a pioneer of participative management, a movement that continues to influence the shape of workplaces around the world. The concept wasn't a grand idea conceived in the CEO's office and imposed on the plant, Harman says. It grew organically out of his going down to Bolivar to, in his words, "put out this fire." Harman's transformation was, above all, a creative one. He had connected two seemingly unrelated ideas and created a radically different approach to management that recognized both the economic and humane benefits of a more collegial workplace. Harman went on to accomplish far more during his career. In addition to founding Harman International, he served as the deputy secretary of commerce under Jimmy Carter. But he always looked back on the incident in Bolivar as the formative event in his professional life, the moment he came into his own as a leader.

The details of Harman's story are unique, but their significance is not. In interviewing more than 40 top leaders in business and the public sector over the past three years, we were surprised to find that all of them—young and old—were able to point to intense, often traumatic, always unplanned experiences that had transformed them and had become the sources of their distinctive leadership abilities. We came to call the experiences that shape leaders "crucibles," after the vessels medieval alchemists used in their attempts to turn base metals into gold. For the leaders we interviewed, the crucible experience was a trial and a test, a point of deep self-reflection that forced them to question who they were and what mattered to them. It required them to examine their values, question their assumptions, hone their judgment. And, invariably, they emerged from the crucible stronger and more sure of themselves and their purpose—changed in some fundamental way.

Leadership crucibles can take many forms. Some are violent, life-threatening events. Others are more prosaic episodes of self-doubt. But whatever the crucible's nature, the people we spoke with were able, like Harman, to create a narrative around it, a story of how they were challenged, met the challenge, and became better leaders. As we studied these stories, we found that they not only told us how individual leaders are shaped but also pointed to some characteristics that seem common to all leaders—characteristics that were formed, or at least exposed, in the crucible.

Learning From Difference

A crucible is, by definition, a transformative experience through which an individual comes to a new or an altered sense of identity. It is perhaps not surprising then that one of the most common types of crucibles we documented involves the experience of prejudice. Being a victim of prejudice is particularly traumatic because it forces an individual to confront a distorted picture of him- or herself, and it often unleashes profound feelings of anger, bewilderment, and even withdrawal. For all its trauma, however, the experience of prejudice is for some a clarifying event. Through it, they gain a clearer vision of who they are, the role they play, and their place in the world.

Consider, for example, Liz Altman, now a Motorola vice president, who was transformed by the year she spent at a Sony camcorder factory in rural Japan, where she faced both estrangement and sexism. It was, says Altman, "by far, the hardest thing I've ever done." The foreign culture particularly its emphasis on groups over individuals was both a shock and a challenge to a young American woman. It wasn't just that she felt lonely in an alien world. She had to face the daunting prospect of carving out a place for herself as the only woman engineer in a plant, and nation, where women usually serve as low-level assistants and clerks known as "office ladies."

Another woman who had come to Japan under similar circumstances had warned Altman that the only way to win the men's respect was to avoid becoming allied with the office ladies. But on her very first morning, when the bell rang for a coffee break, the men headed in one direction and the women in another and the women saved her a place at their table, while the men ignored her. Instinct told Altman to ignore the warning rather than insult the women by rebuffing their invitation.

Over the next few days, she continued to join the women during breaks, a choice that gave her a comfortable haven from which to observe the unfamiliar office culture. But it didn't take her long to notice that some of the men spent the break at their desks reading magazines, and Altman determined that she could do the same on occasion. Finally, after paying close attention to the conversations around her, she learned that several of the men were interested in mountain biking. Because Altman wanted to buy a mountain bike, she approached them for advice. Thus, over time, she established herself as something of a free agent, sometimes sitting with the women and other times engaging with the men.

And as it happened, one of the women she'd sat with on her very first day, the department secretary, was married to one of the engineers. The secretary took it upon herself to include Altman in social gatherings, a turn of events that probably wouldn't have occurred if Altman had alienated her female coworkers on that first day. "Had I just gone to try to break in with [the men] and not had her as an ally, it would never have happened," she says.

Looking back, Altman believes the experience greatly helped her gain a clearer sense of her personal strengths and capabilities, preparing her for other difficult situations. Her tenure in Japan taught her to observe closely and to avoid jumping to conclusions based on cultural assumptions invaluable skills in her current position at Motorola, where she leads efforts to smooth alliances with other corporate cultures, including those of Motorola's different regional operations.

Altman has come to believe that she wouldn't have been as able to do the Motorola job if she hadn't lived in a foreign country and experienced the dissonance of cultures:" even if you're sitting in the same room, ostensibly agreeing...unless you understand the frame of reference, you're probably missing a bunch of what's going on." Altman also credits her crucible with building her confidence she feels that she can cope with just about anything that comes her way.

People can feel the stigma of cultural differences much closer to home, as well. Muriel ("Mickie") Siebert, the first woman to own a seat on the New York Stock Exchange, found her crucible on the Wall Street of the 1950s and 1960s, an arena so sexist that she couldn't get a job as a stockbroker until she took her first name off her résumé and substituted a genderless initial. Other than the secretaries and the occasional analyst, women were few and far between. That she was Jewish was another strike against her at a time, she points out, when most of big business was "not nice" to either women or Jews. But Siebert wasn't broken or defeated. Instead, she emerged stronger, more focused, and more determined to change the status quo that excluded her.

When we interviewed Siebert, she described her way of addressing anti-Semitism a technique that quieted the offensive comments of her peers without destroying the relationships she needed to do her job effectively. According to Siebert, at the time it was part of doing business to have a few drinks at lunch. She remembers, "Give somebody a couple of drinks, and they would talk about the Jews." She had a greeting card she used for those occasions that went like this: Roses are reddish, Violets are bluish, In case you don't know, I am Jewish.

Siebert would have the card hand-delivered to the person who had made the anti-Semitic remarks, and on the card she had written, "Enjoyed lunch." As she recounts, "They got that card in the afternoon, and I never had to take any of that nonsense again. And I never embarrassed anyone, either." It was because she was unable to get credit for the business she was bringing in at any of the large Wall Street firms that she bought a seat on the New York Stock Exchange and started working for herself.

In subsequent years, she went on to found Muriel Siebert & Company (now Siebert Financial Corporation) and has dedicated herself to helping other people avoid some of the difficulties she faced as a young professional. A prominent advocate for women in business and a leader in developing financial products directed at women, she's also devoted to educating children about financial opportunities and responsibility.

We didn't interview lawyer and presidential adviser Vernon Jordan for this article, but he, too, offers a powerful reminder of how prejudice can prove transformational rather than debilitating. In Vernon Can Read! A Memoir (Public Affairs, 2001), Jordan describes the vicious baiting he was subjected to as a young man. The man who treated him in this offensive way was his employer, Robert F. Maddox. Jordan served the racist former mayor of Atlanta at dinner, in a white jacket, with a napkin over his arm. He also functioned as Maddox's chauffeur. Whenever Maddox could, he would derisively announce, "Vernon can read!" as if the literacy of a young African-American were a source of wonderment.

Subjected to this type of abuse, a lesser man might have allowed Maddox to destroy him. But in his memoir, Jordan gives his own interpretation of Maddox's sadistic heckling, a tale that empowered Jordan instead of embittering him. When he looked at Maddox through the rearview mirror, Jordan did not see a powerful member of Georgia's ruling class. He saw a desperate anachronism, a person who lashed out because he knew his time was up. As Jordan writes about Maddox, "His half-mocking, half-serious comments about my education were the death rattle of his culture. When he saw that I was...crafting a life for myself that would make me a man in...ways he thought of as being a man, he was deeply unnerved."

Maddox's cruelty was the crucible that, consciously or not, Jordan imbued with redemptive meaning. Instead of lashing out or being paralyzed with hatred, Jordan saw the fall of the Old South and imagined his own future freed of the historical shackles of racism. His ability to organize meaning around a potential crisis turned it into the crucible around which his leadership was forged.

Prevailing over Darkness

Some crucible experiences illuminate a hidden and suppressed area of the soul. These are often among the harshest of crucibles, involving, for instance, episodes of illness or violence. In the case of Sidney Rittenberg, the crucible took the form of 16 years of unjust imprisonment, in solitary confinement, in Communist China. In 1949 Rittenberg was initially jailed, without explanation, by former friends in Chairman Mao Zedong's government and spent his first year in total darkness when he wasn't being interrogated. (Rittenberg later learned that his arrest came at the behest of Communist Party officials in Moscow, who had wrongly identified him as a CIA agent.) Thrown into jail, confined to a tiny, pitch-dark cell, Rittenberg did not rail or panic. Instead, within minutes, he remembered a stanza of verse, four lines recited to him when he was a small child:

They drew a circle that shut me out, Heretic, rebel, a thing to flout. But love and I had the wit to win, We drew a circle that took them in! That bit of verse (adapted from "Outwitted," a poem by Edwin Markham) was the key to Rittenberg's survival. "My God," he thought, "there's my strategy." He drew the prison guards into his circle, developing relationships that would help him adapt to his confinement. Fluent in Chinese, he persuaded the guards to deliver him books and, eventually, provide a candle so that he could read. He also decided, after his first year, to devote himself to improving his mind making it more scientific, more pure, and more dedicated to socialism. He believed that if he raised his consciousness, his captors would understand him better. And when, over time, the years in the dark began to take an intellectual toll on him and he found his reason faltering, he could still summon fairy tales and childhood stories such as The Little Engine That Could and take comfort from their simple messages. By contrast, many of Rittenberg's fellow prisoners either lashed out in anger or withdrew. "They tended to go up the wall...They couldn't make it. And I think the reason was that they didn't understand...that happiness...is not a function of your circumstances; it's a function of your outlook on life."

Rittenberg's commitment to his ideals continued upon his release. His cell door opened suddenly in 1955, after his first six-year term in prison. He recounts, "Here was a representative of the central government telling me that I had been wronged, that the government was making a formal apology to me...and that they would do everything possible to make restitution." When his captors offered him money to start a new life in the United States or to travel in Europe, Rittenberg declined, choosing instead to stay in China and continue his work for the Communist Party.

And even after a second arrest, which put him into solitary confinement for ten years as retaliation for his support of open democracy during the Cultural Revolution, Rittenberg did not allow his spirit to be broken. Instead, he used his time in prison as an opportunity to question his belief system in particular, his commitment to Marxism and Chairman Mao.

"In that sense, prison emancipated me," he says. Rittenberg studied, read, wrote, and thought, and he learned something about himself in the process: "I realized I had this great fear of being a turncoat, which...was so powerful that it prevented me from even looking at Even to question was an act of betrayal. After I got out...the scales fell away from my eyes and I understood that...the basic doctrine of arriving at democracy through dictatorship was wrong."

What's more, Rittenberg emerged from prison certain that absolutely nothing in his professional life could break him and went on to start a company with his wife. Rittenberg Associates is a consulting firm dedicated to developing business ties between the United States and China. Today, Rittenberg is as committed to his ideals—if not to his view of the best way to get there as he was 50 years ago, when he was so severely tested.

Meeting Great Expectations

Fortunately, not all crucible experiences are traumatic. In fact, they can involve a positive, if deeply challenging, experience such as having a demanding boss or mentor. Judge Nathaniel R. Jones of the U.S. Court of Appeals for the Sixth Circuit, for instance, attributes much of his success to his interaction with a splendid mentor. That mentor was J. Maynard Dickerson, a successful attorney the first black city prosecutor in the United States and editor of a local African-American newspaper.

Dickerson influenced Jones at many levels. For instance, the older man brought Jones behind the scenes to witness firsthand the great civil rights struggle of the 1950s, inviting him to sit in on conversations with activists like Thurgood Marshall, Walter White, Roy Wilkins, and Robert C. Weaver. Says Jones, "I was struck by their resolve, their humor and their determination not to let the system define them. Rather than just feel beaten down, they turned it around." The experience no doubt influenced the many important opinions Judge Jones has written in regard to civil rights.

Dickerson was both model and coach. His lessons covered every aspect of Jones's intellectual growth and presentation of self, including schooling in what we now call "emotional intelligence." Dickerson set the highest standards for Jones, especially in the area of communication skills a facility we've found essential to leadership. Dickerson edited Jones's early attempts at writing a sports column with respectful ruthlessness, in red ink, as Jones remembers to this day marking up the copy so that it looked, as Jones says, "like something chickens had a fight over." But Dickerson also took the time to explain every single mistake and why it mattered.

His mentor also expected the teenage Jones to speak correctly at all times and would hiss discreetly in his direction if he stumbled. Great expectations are evidence of great respect, and as Jones learned all the complex, often subtle lessons of how to succeed, he was motivated in no small measure by his desire not to disappoint the man he still calls "Mr. Dickerson." Dickerson gave Jones the kind of intensive mentoring that was tantamount to grooming him for a kind of professional and moral succession and Jones has indeed become an instrument for the profound societal change for which Dickerson fought so courageously as well. Jones found life-changing meaning in the attention Dickerson paid to him attention fueled by a conviction that he, too, though only a teenager, had a vital role to play in society and an important destiny.

Another story of a powerful mentor came to us from Michael Klein, a young man who made millions in Southern California real estate while still in his teens, only to lose it by the time he turned 20 and then go on to start several other businesses. His mentor was his grandfather Max S. Klein, who created the paint-by-numbers fad that swept the United States in the 1950s and 1960s. Klein was only four or five years old when his grandfather approached him and offered to share his business expertise. Over the years, Michael Klein's grandfather taught him to learn from and to cope with change, and the two spoke by phone for an hour every day until shortly before Max Klein's death.

The Essentials of Leadership

In our interviews, we heard many other stories of crucible experiences. Take Jack Coleman, 78-year-old former president of Haverford College in Pennsylvania. He told us of one day, during the Vietnam War, when he heard that a group of students was planning to pull down the American flag and burn it and that former members of the school's football team were going to make sure the students didn't succeed. Seemingly out of nowhere, Coleman had the idea to preempt the violence by suggesting that the protesting students take down the flag, wash it, and then put it back up a crucible moment that even now elicits tremendous emotion in Coleman as he describes that day.

There's also Common Cause founder John W. Gardner, who died earlier this year at 89. He identified his arduous training as a Marine during World War II as the crucible in which his leadership abilities emerged. Architect Frank Gehry spoke of the biases he experienced as a Jew in college. Jeff Wilke, a general manager at a major manufacturer, told us of the day he learned that an employee had been killed in his plant an experience that taught him that leadership was about much more than making quarterly numbers.

So, what allowed these people to not only cope with these difficult situations but also learn from them? We believe that great leaders possess four essential skills, and, we were surprised to learn, these happen to be the same skills that allow a person to find meaning in what could be a debilitating experience. First is the ability to engage others in shared meaning. Consider Sidney Harman, who dived into a chaotic work environment to mobilize employees around an entirely new approach to management. Second is a distinctive and compelling voice. Look at Jack Coleman's ability to defuse a potentially violent situation with only his words. Third is a sense of integrity (including a strong set of values). Here, we point again to Coleman, whose values prevailed even during the emotionally charged clash between peace demonstrators and the angry (and strong) former football team members.

But by far the most critical skill of the four is what we call "adaptive capacity." This is, in essence, applied creativity an almost magical ability to transcend adversity, with all its attendant stresses, and to emerge stronger than before. It's composed of two primary qualities: the ability to grasp context, and hardiness. The ability to grasp context implies an ability to weigh a welter of factors, ranging from how very different groups of people will interpret a gesture to being able to put a situation in perspective. Without this, leaders are utterly lost, because they cannot connect with their constituents. M. Douglas Ivester, who succeeded Roberto Goizueta at Coca-Cola, exhibited a woeful inability to grasp context, lasting just 28 months on the job. For example, he demoted his highest-ranked African-American employee even as the company was losing a $200 million class-action suit brought by black employees and this in Atlanta, a city with a powerful African-American majority. Contrast Ivester with Vernon Jordan. Jordan realized his boss's time was up not just his time in power, but the era that formed him. And so Jordan was able to see past the insults and recognize his boss's bitterness for what it was desperate lashing out.

Hardiness is just what it sounds like the perseverance and toughness that enable people to emerge from devastating circumstances without losing hope. Look at Michael Klein, who experienced failure but didn't let it defeat him. He found himself with a single asset a tiny software company he'd acquired. Klein built it into Transoft Networks, which Hewlett-

Packard acquired in 1999. Consider, too, Mickie Siebert, who used her sense of humor to curtail offensive conversations. Or Sidney Rittenberg's strength during his imprisonment. He drew on his personal memories and inner strength to emerge from his lengthy prison term without bitterness.

It is the combination of hardiness and ability to grasp context that, above all, allows a person to not only survive an ordeal, but to learn from it, and to emerge stronger, more engaged, and more committed than ever. These attributes allow leaders to grow from their crucibles, instead of being destroyed by them to find opportunity where others might find only despair. This is the stuff of true leadership.

Geeks and Geezers

We didn't set out to learn about crucibles. Our research for this article and for our new book, Geeks and Geezers, was actually designed to uncover the ways that era influences a leader's motivation and aspirations. We interviewed 43 of to day's top leaders in business and the public sector, limiting our subjects to people born in or before 1925, or in or after 1970. To our delight, we learned a lot about how age and era affect leadership style.

Our geeks and geezers (the affection ate shorthand we eventually used to describe the two groups) had very different ideas about paying your dues, work-life balance, the role of heroes, and more. But they also shared some striking similarities among them a love of learning and strong sense of values.

Most intriguing, though, both our geeks and our geezers told us again and again how certain experiences inspired them, shaped them, and, indeed, taught them to lead. And so, as the best research often does, our work turned out to be even more interesting than we thought it would be. We continued to explore the influences of era our findings are described in our book but at the same time we probed for stories of these crucible experiences. These are the stories we share with you here.

Reinvention in the Extreme: The Power of Neoteny

All of our interview subjects described their crucibles as opportunities for reinvention for taking stock of their lives and finding meaning in circumstances many people would see as daunting and potentially incapacitating. In the extreme, this capacity for reinvention comes to resemble eternal youth a kind of vigor, openness, and an enduring capacity for wonder that is the antithesis of stereotyped old age.

We borrowed a term from biology "neoteny," which, according to the American Heritage Dictionary, means "retention of juvenile characteristics in the adults of a species" to describe this quality, this delight in life long learning, which every leader we interviewed displayed, regardless of age. To a person, they were full of energy, curiosity, and confidence that the world is a place of wonders spread before them like an endless feast. Robert Galvin, former Motorola chairman now in his late 70s, spends his weekends windsurfing. Arthur Levitt, Jr., former SEC chairman who turned 71 this year, is an avid Outward Bound trekker. And architect Frank Gehry is now a 72-year-old ice hockey player.

But it's not only an affinity for physical activity that characterizes neoteny it's an appetite for learning and self-development, a curiosity and passion for life.

To understand why this quality is so powerful in a leader, it might help to take a quick look at the scientific principle behind it neoteny as an evolutionary engine. It is the winning, puppyish quality of certain ancient wolves that allowed them to evolve into dogs.

Over thousands of years, humans favored wolves that were the friendliest, most approachable, and most curious. Naturally, people were most drawn to the wolves least likely to attack without warning, that readily locked eyes with them, and that seemed almost human in their eager response to people; the ones, in short, that stayed the most like puppies. Like human infants, they have certain physical qualities that elicit a nurturing response in human adults.

When infants see an adult, they often respond with a smile that begins small and slowly grows into a radiant grin that makes the adult feel at center of the universe. Recent studies of bonding indicate that nursing and other intimate interactions with an infant cause the mother's system to be flooded with oxytocin, a calming, feel-good hormone that is a powerful antidote to cortisol, the hormone produced by stress. Oxytocin appears to be the glue that produces bonding. And the baby's distinctive look and behaviors cause oxytocin to be released in the fortunate adult. That appearance the one that pulls an involuntary "aaah" out of us whenever we see a baby and those oxytocin-inducing behaviors allow infants to recruit adults to be their nurturers, essential if such vulnerable and incompletely developed creatures are to survive.

The power of neoteny to recruit protectors and nurturers was vividly illustrated in the former Soviet Union. Forty years ago, a So viet scientist decided to start breeding silver foxes for neoteny at a Siberian fur farm. The goal was to create a tamer fox that would go with less fuss to slaughter than the typical silver fox. Only the least aggressive, most approachable animals were bred.

The experiment continued for 40 years, and today, after 35 generations, the farm is home to a breed of tame foxes that look and act more like juvenile foxes and even dogs than like their wild forebears. The physical changes in the animals are remarkable (some have floppy, dog-like ears), but what is truly stunning is the change neoteny has wrought in the human response to them. Instead of taking advantage of the fact that these neotenic animals don't snap and snarl on the way to their deaths, their human keepers appear to have been recruited by their newly cute and endearing charges. The keepers and the foxes appear to have formed close bonds, so close that the keepers are trying to find ways to save the animals from slaughter.

The Idea in Brief

What enables one leader to inspire confidence, loyalty, and hard work, while others with equal vision and intelligence stumble? How individuals deal with adversity provides a clue.

Extraordinary leaders find meaning in and learn from the most negative events. Like phoenixes rising from the ashes, they emerge from adversity stronger, more confident in themselves and their purpose, and more committed to their work. Such transformative events are called crucibles —a severe test or trial. Crucibles are intense, often traumatic and always unplanned

THE CRUCIBLE EXPERIENCE

Crucibles force leaders into deep self-reflection, where they examine their values, question their assumptions, and hone their judgment.

Example: Sidney Harman—co-founder of audio components company Harman Kardon and president of an experimental college encouraging student-driven education encountered his crucible when "all hell broke loose" in one of his factories. After managers postponed a scheduled break because the buzzer didn't sound, workers rebelled. "I don't work for no buzzer," one proclaimed.

To Harman, this refusal to bow to management's senseless rule suggested a surprising link between student-driven education and business. Pioneering participative management, Harman transformed his plant into a kind of campus, offering classes and encouraging dissent. He considers the rebellion the formative event in his career the moment he became a true leader.

THE MANY SHAPES OF CRUCIBLES

Some crucibles are violent and life-threatening (encounters with prejudice, illness); others are more positive, yet profoundly challenging (such as demanding bosses or mentors). Whatever the shape, leaders create a narrative telling how they met the challenge and became better for it.

Example: While working for former Atlanta mayor Robert F. Maddox, Vernon Jordan endured repeated racial heckling from Maddox. Rather than letting Maddox's sadism destroy him, Jordan interpreted the behavior as a desperate lashing out by someone who knew the era of the Old South was ending. Jordan's response empowered him to become an esteemed lawyer and presidential advisor.

ESSENTIAL LEADERSHIP SKILLS

Four skills enable leaders to learn from adversity:

1. Engage others in shared meaning. For example, Sidney Harman mobilized employees around a radical new management approach amid a factory crisis.

2. A distinctive, compelling voice. With words alone, college president Jack Coleman preempted a violent clash between the football team and anti-Vietnam War demonstrators threatening to burn the American flag. Coleman's suggestion to the protestors? Lower the flag, wash it, then put it back up.

3. Integrity. Coleman's values prevailed during the emotionally charged face-off between antiwar demonstrators and irate football players.

4. Adaptive capacity. This most critical skill includes the ability to grasp context , and hardiness. Grasping context requires weighing many factors (e.g., how different people will interpret a gesture). Without this quality, leaders can't connect with constituents.

Hardiness provides the perseverance and toughness needed to remain hopeful despite disaster. For instance, Michael Klein made millions in real estate during his teens, lost it all by age 20—then built several more businesses, including transforming a tiny software company into a Hewlett-Packard acquisition.

CHAPTER 3

How to Manage Your Boss

If you forge ties with your boss based on mutual respect and understanding, both of you will be more effective.
by John J. Gabarro and John P. Kotter

To many people, the phrase "managing your boss" may sound unusual or suspicious. Because of the traditional top-down emphasis in most organizations, it is not obvious why you need to manage relationships upward—unless, of course, you would do so for personal or political reasons. But we are not referring to political maneuvering or to apple polishing. We are using the term to mean the process of consciously working with your superior to obtain the best possible results for you, your boss, and the company.

Recent studies suggest that effective managers take time and effort to manage not only relationships with their subordinates but also those with their bosses. These studies also show that this essential aspect of management is sometimes ignored by otherwise talented and aggressive managers. Indeed, some managers who actively and effectively supervise subordinates, products, markets, and technolo gies assume an almost passively reactive stance vis-à-vis their bosses. Such a stance almost always hurts them and their companies.

If you doubt the importance of managing your relationship with your boss or how difficult it is to do so effectively, consider for a moment the following sad but telling story:

Frank Gibbons was an acknowledged manufacturing genius in his industry and, by any profitability standard, a very effective executive. In 1973, his strengths propelled him into the position of vice president of manufacturing for the second largest and most profitable company in its industry. Gibbons was not, however, a good manager of people. He knew this, as did others in his company and his industry. Recognizing this weakness, the president made sure that those who reported to Gibbons were good at working with people and could compensate for his limitations. The arrangement worked well.

In 1975, Philip Bonnevie was promoted into a position reporting to Gibbons. In keeping with the previous pattern, the president selected Bonnevie because he had an excellent track record and a reputation for being good with people. In making that selection, however, the president neglected to notice that, in his rapid rise through the organization, Bonnevie had always had goodto-excellent bosses. He had never been forced to manage a relationship with a difficult boss. In retrospect, Bonnevie admits he had never thought that managing his boss was a part of his job.

Fourteen months after he started working for Gibbons, Bonnevie was fired. During that same quarter, the company reported a net loss for the first time in seven years. Many of those who were close to these events say that they don't really understand what happened. This much is known, however: While the company was bringing out a major new product— a process that required sales, engineering, and manufacturing groups to coordinate decisions very carefully—a whole series of misunderstandings and bad feelings developed between Gibbons and Bonnevie.

For example, Bonnevie claims Gibbons was aware of and had accepted Bonnevie's decision to use a new type of machinery to make the new product; Gibbons swears he did not. Furthermore, Gibbons claims he made it clear to Bonnevie that the introduction of the product was too important to the company in the short run to take any major risks.

As a result of such misunderstandings, planning went awry: A new manufacturing plant was built that could not produce the new product designed by engineering, in the volume desired by sales, at a cost agreed on by the executive committee. Gibbons blamed Bonnevie for the mistake. Bonnevie blamed Gibbons.

Of course, one could argue that the problem here was caused by Gibbons's inability to manage his subordinates. But one can make just as strong a case that the problem was related to Bonnevie's inability to manage his boss. Remember, Gibbons was not having difficulty with any other subordinates. Moreover, given the personal price paid by Bonnevie (being fired and having his reputation within the industry severely tarnished), there was little consolation in saying the problem was that Gibbons was poor at managing subordinates. Everyone already knew that.

We believe that the situation could have turned out differently had Bonnevie been more adept at understanding Gibbons and at managing his relationship with him. In this case, an inability to manage upward was unusually costly. The company lost $2 million to $5 million, and Bonnevie's career was, at least temporarily, disrupted. Many less costly cases similar to this probably occur regularly in all major corporations, and the cumulative effect can be very destructive.

Misreading the Boss–Subordinate Relationship

People often dismiss stories like the one we just related as being merely cases of personality conflict. Because two people can on occasion be psychologically or temperamentally incapable of working together, this can be an apt description. But more often, we have found, a personality conflict is only a part of the problem—sometimes a very small part.

Bonnevie did not just have a different personality from Gibbons, he also made or had unrealistic assumptions and expectations about the very nature of boss–subordinate relationships. Specifically, he did not recognize that his relationship to Gibbons involved *mutual dependence* between two *fallible* human beings. Failing to recognize this, a manager typically either avoids trying to manage his or her relationship with a boss or manages it ineffectively.

Some people behave as if their bosses were not very dependent on them. They fail to see how much the boss needs their help and cooperation to do his or her job effectively. These people refuse to acknowledge that the boss can be severely hurt by their actions and needs cooperation, dependability, and honesty from them.

Some people see themselves as not very dependent on their bosses. They gloss over how much help and information they need from the boss in order to perform their own jobs well. This superficial view is particularly damaging when a manager's job and decisions affect other parts of the organization, as was the case in Bonnevie's situation. A manager's immediate boss can play a critical role in linking the manager to the rest of the organization, making sure the manager's priorities are consistent with organizational needs, and in securing the resources the manager needs to perform well. Yet some managers need to see themselves as practically self-sufficient, as not needing the critical information and resources a boss can supply.

Many managers, like Bonnevie, assume that the boss will magically know what information or help their subordinates need and provide it to them. Certainly, some bosses do an excellent job of caring for their subordinates in this way, but for a manager to expect that from all bosses is dangerously unrealistic. A more reasonable expectation for managers to have is that modest help will be forthcoming. After all, bosses are only human. Most really effective managers accept this fact and assume primary responsibility for their own careers and development. They make a point of seeking the information and help they need to do a job instead of waiting for their bosses to provide it.

In light of the foregoing, it seems to us that managing a situation of mutual dependence among fallible human beings requires the following:

1. You have a good understanding of the other person and yourself, especially regarding strengths, weaknesses, work styles, and needs.

2. You use this information to develop and manage a healthy working relationship—one that is compatible with both people's work styles and assets, is characterized by mutual expectations, and meets the most critical needs of the other person.

This combination is essentially what we have found highly effective managers doing.

Understanding the Boss

Managing your boss requires that you gain an understanding of the boss and his or her context, as well as your own situation. All managers do this to some degree, but many are not thorough enough.

At a minimum, you need to appreciate your boss's goals and pressures, his or her strengths and weaknesses. What are your boss's organizational and personal objectives, and what are his or her pressures, especially those from his or her own boss and others at the same level? What are your boss's long suits and blind spots? What is the preferred style of working? Does your boss like to get information through memos, formal meetings, or phone calls? Does he or she thrive on conflict or try to minimize it? Without this information, a manager is flying blind when dealing with the boss, and unnecessary conflicts, misunderstandings, and problems are inevitable.

In one situation we studied, a top-notch marketing manager with a superior performance record was hired into a company as a vice president "to straighten out the marketing and sales problems." The company, which was having financial difficulties, had recently been acquired by a larger corporation. The president was eager to turn it around and gave the new marketing vice president free rein—at least initially. Based on his previous experience, the new vice president correctly diagnosed that greater market share was needed for the company and that strong product management was required to bring that about. Following that logic, he made a number of pricing decisions aimed at increasing high-volume business.

When margins declined and the financial situation did not improve, however, the president increased pressure on the new vice president. Believing that the situation would eventually correct itself as the company gained back market share, the vice president resisted the pressure.

When by the second quarter, margins and profits had still failed to improve, the president took direct control over all pricing decisions and put all items on a set level of margin, regardless of volume. The new vice president began to find himself shut out by the president, and their relationship deteriorated. In fact, the vice president found the president's behavior bizarre. Unfortunately, the president's new pricing scheme also failed to increase margins, and by the fourth quarter, both the president and the vice president were fired.

What the new vice president had not known until it was too late was that improving marketing and sales had been only *one* of the president's goals. His most immediate goal had been to make the company more profitable quickly.

Nor had the new vice president known that his boss was invested in this short-term priority for personal as well as business reasons. The president had been a strong advocate of the acquisition within the parent company, and his personal credibility was at stake.

The vice president made three basic errors. He took information supplied to him at face value, he made assumptions in areas where he had no information, and—what was most damaging—he never actively tried to clarify what his boss's objectives were. As a result, he ended up taking actions that were actually at odds with the president's priorities and objectives.

Managers who work effectively with their bosses do not behave this way. They seek out information about the boss's goals and problems and pressures. They are alert for opportunities to question the boss and others around him or her to test their assumptions. They pay attention to clues in the boss's behavior. Although it is imperative that they do this especially when they begin working with a new boss, effective managers also do this on an ongoing basis because they recognize that priorities and concerns change.

Being sensitive to a boss's work style can be crucial, especially when the boss is new. For example, a new president who was organized and formal in his approach replaced a man who was informal and intuitive. The new president worked best when he had written reports. He also preferred formal meetings with set agendas.

One of his division managers realized this need and worked with the new president to identify the kinds and frequency of information and reports that the president wanted. This manager also made a point of sending background information and brief agendas ahead of time for their discussions. He found that with this type of preparation their meetings were very useful. Another interesting result was, he found that with adequate preparation his new boss was even more effective at brainstorming problems than his more informal and intuitive predecessor had been.

In contrast, another division manager never fully understood how the new boss's work style differed from that of his predecessor. To the degree that he did sense it, he experienced it as too much control. As a result, he seldom sent the new president the background information he needed, and the president never felt fully prepared for meetings with the manager. In fact, the president spent much of the time when they met trying to get information that he felt he should have had earlier. The boss experienced these meetings as frustrating and inefficient, and the subordinate often found himself thrown off guard by the questions that the president asked. Ultimately, this division manager resigned.

The difference between the two division managers just described was not so much one of ability or even adaptability. Rather, one of the men was more sensitive to his boss's work style and to the implications of his boss's needs than the other was.

Understanding Yourself

The boss is only one-half of the relationship. You are the other half, as well as the part over which you have more direct control. Developing an effective working relationship requires, then, that you know your own needs, strengths and weaknesses, and personal style.

You are not going to change either your basic personality structure or that of your boss. But you can become aware of what it is about you that impedes or facilitates working with your boss and, with that awareness, take actions that make the relationship more effective.

For example, in one case we observed, a manager and his superior ran into problems whenever they disagreed. The boss's typical response was to harden his position and overstate it. The manager's reaction was then to raise the ante and intensify the for cefulness of his argument. In doing this, he channeled his anger into sharpening his attacks on the logical fallacies he saw in his boss's assumptions. His boss in turn would become even more adamant about holding his original position. Pre dictably, this escalating cycle resulted in the subordinate avoiding whenever possible any topic of potential conflict with his boss.

In discussing this problem with his peers, the manager discovered that his reaction to the boss was typical of how he generally reacted to counterarguments—but with a difference. His response would overwhelm his peers but not his boss. Because his attempts to discuss this problem with his boss were unsuccessful, he concluded that the only way to change the situation was to deal with his own instinctive reactions. Whenever the two reached an impasse, he would check his own impatience and suggest that they break up and think about it before getting together again. Usually when they renewed their discussion, they had digested their differences and were more able to work them through.

Gaining this level of self-awareness and acting on it are difficult but not impossible. For example, by reflecting over his past experiences, a young manager learned that he was not very good at dealing with difficult and emotional issues where people were involved. Because he disliked those issues and realized that his instinctive responses to them were seldom very good, he developed a habit of touching base with his boss whenever such a problem arose. Their discussions always surfaced ideas and approaches the manager had not considered. In many cases, they also identified specific actions the boss could take to help.

Although a superior–subordinate relationship is one of mutual dependence, it is also one in which the subordinate is typically more dependent on the boss than the other way around. This dependence inevitably results in the subordinate feeling a certain degree of frustration, sometimes anger, when his actions or options are constrained by his boss's decisions. This is a normal part of life and occurs in the best of relationships. The way in which a manager handles these frustrations largely depends on his or her predisposition toward dependence on authority figures.

Some people's instinctive reaction under these circumstances is to resent the boss's authority and to rebel against the boss's decisions. Sometimes a person will escalate a conflict beyond what is appropriate. Seeing the boss almost as an institutional enemy, this type of manager will often, without being conscious of it, fight with the boss just for the sake of fighting. The subordinate's reactions to being constrained are usually strong and sometimes impulsive. He or she sees the boss as someone who, by virtue of the role, is a hindrance to progress, an obstacle to be circumvented or at best tolerated.

Psychologists call this pattern of reactions counterdependent behavior. Although a counterdependent person is difficult for most superiors to manage and usually has a history of strained relationships with superiors, this sort of manager is apt to have even more trouble with a boss who tends to be directive or authoritarian. When the manager acts on his or her negative feelings, often in subtle and nonverbal ways, the boss sometimes does become the enemy. Sensing the subordinate's latent hostility, the boss will lose trust in the subordinate or his or her judgment and then behave even less openly.

Paradoxically, a manager with this type of predisposition is often a good manager of his or her own people. He or she will many times go out of the way to get support for them and will not hesitate to go to bat for them.

At the other extreme are managers who swallow their anger and behave in a very compliant fashion when the boss makes what they know to be a poor decision. These managers will agree with the boss even when a disagreement might be welcome or when the boss would easily alter a decision if given more information. Because they bear no relationship to the specific situation at hand, their responses are as much an overreaction as those of counterdependent managers. Instead of seeing the boss as an enemy, these people deny their anger—the other extreme—and tend to see the boss as if he or she were an all-wise parent who should know best, should take responsibility for their careers, train them in all they need to know, and protect them from overly ambitious peers.

Both counterdependence and overdependence lead managers to hold unrealistic views of what a boss is. Both views ignore that bosses, like everyone else, are imperfect and fallible. They don't have unlimited time, encyclopedic knowledge, or extrasensory perception; nor are they evil enemies. They have their own pressures and concerns that are sometimes at odds with the wishes of the subordinate and often for good reason.

Altering predispositions toward authority, especially at the extremes, is almost impossible without intensive psychotherapy (psychoanalytic theory and research suggest that such predispositions are deeply rooted in a person's personality and upbringing). However, an awareness of these extremes and the range between them can be very useful in understanding where your own predispositions fall and what the implications are for how you tend to behave in relation to your boss.

If you believe, on the one hand, that you have some tendencies toward counterdependence, you can understand and even predict what your reactions and overreactions are likely to be. If, on the other hand, you believe you have some tendencies toward overdependence, you might question the extent to which your overcompliance or inability to confront real differences may be making both you and your boss less effective.

Developing and Managing the Relationship

With a clear understanding of both your boss and yourself, you can *usually* establish a way of working together that fits both of you, that is characterized by unambiguous mutual expectations, and that helps you both be more productive and effective. The "Checklist for Managing Your Boss summarizes some things such a relationship consists of. Following are a few more.

Compatible Work Styles. Above all else, a good working relationship with a boss accommodates differences in work style. For example, in one situation we studied, a manager (who had a relatively good relationship with his superior) realized that during meetings his boss would often become inattentive and sometimes brusque. The subordinate's own style tended to be discursive and exploratory. He would often digress from the topic at hand to deal with background factors, alternative approaches, and so forth. His boss preferred to discuss problems with a minimum of background detail and became impatient and distracted whenever his subordinate digressed from the immediate issue.

Recognizing this difference in style, the manager became terser and more direct during meetings with his boss. To help himself do this, before meetings, he would develop brief agendas that he used as a guide. Whenever he felt that a digression was needed, he explained why. This small shift in his own style made these meetings more effective and far less frustrating for both of them.

Subordinates can adjust their styles in response to their bosses' preferred method for receiving information. Peter Drucker divides bosses into "listeners" and "readers." Some bosses like to get information in report form so they can read and study it. Others work better with information and reports presented in person so they can ask questions. As Drucker points out, the implications are obvious. If your boss is a listener, you brief him or her in person, *then* follow it up with a memo. If your boss is a reader, you cover important items or proposals in a memo or report, *then* discuss them.

Other adjustments can be made according to a boss's decision-making style. Some bosses prefer to be involved in decisions and problems as they arise. These are high-involvement managers who like to keep their hands on the pulse of the operation. Usually their needs (and your own) are best satisfied if you touch base with them on an ad hoc basis. A boss who has a need to be involved will become involved one way or another, so there are advantages to including him or her at your initiative. Other bosses prefer to delegate—they don't want to be involved. They expect you to come to them with major problems and inform them about any important changes.

Creating a compatible relationship also involves drawing on each other's strengths and making up for each other's weaknesses. Because he knew that the boss—the vice president of engineering—was not very good at monitoring his employees' problems, one manager we studied made a point of doing it himself. The stakes were high: The engineers and technicians were all union members, the company worked on a customer-contract basis, and the company had recently experienced a serious strike.

The manager worked closely with his boss, along with people in the scheduling department and the personnel office, to make sure that potential problems were avoided. He also developed an informal arrangement through which his boss would review with him any proposed changes in personnel or assignment policies before taking action. The boss valued his advice and credited his subordinate for improving both the performance of the division and the labor–management climate.

Mutual Expectations. The subordinate who passively assumes that he or she knows what the boss expects is in for trouble. Of course, some superiors will spell out their expectations very explicitly and in great detail. But most do not. And although many corporations have systems that provide a basis for communicating expectations (such as formal planning processes, career planning reviews, and performance appraisal reviews), these systems never work perfectly. Also, between these formal reviews, expectations invariably change.

Ultimately, the burden falls on the subordinate to find out what the boss's expectations are. They can be both broad (such as what kinds of problems the boss wishes to be informed about and when) as well as very specific (such things as when a particular project should be completed and what kinds of information the boss needs in the interim).

Getting a boss who tends to be vague or not explicit to express expectations can be difficult. But effective managers find ways to get that information. Some will draft a detailed memo covering key aspects of their work and then send it to their boss for approval. They then follow this up with a face-to-face discussion in which they go over each item in the memo. A discussion like this will often surface virtually all of the boss's expectations.

Other effective managers will deal with an inexplicit boss by initiating an ongoing series of informal discussions about "good management" and "our objectives." Still others find useful information more indirectly through those who used to work for the boss and through the formal planning systems in which the boss makes commitments to his or her own superior. Which approach you choose, of course, should depend on your understanding of your boss's style.

Developing a workable set of mutual expectations also requires that you communicate your own expectations to the boss, find out if they are realistic, and influence the boss to accept the ones that are important to you. Being able to influence the boss to value your expectations can be particularly important if the boss is an overachiever. Such a boss will often set unrealistically high standards that need to be brought into line with reality.

A Flow of Information. How much information a boss needs about what a subordinate is doing will vary significantly depending on the boss's style, the situation he or she is in, and the confidence the boss has in the subordinate. But it is not uncommon for a boss to need more information than the subordinate would naturally supply or for the subordinate to think the boss knows more than he or she really does. Effective managers recognize that they probably underestimate what their bosses need to know and make sure they find ways to keep them informed through processes that fit their styles.

Managing the flow of information upward is particularly difficult if the boss does not like to hear about problems. Although many people would deny it, bosses often give off signals that they want to hear only good news. They show great displeasure—usually nonverbally—when someone tells them about a problem. Ignoring individual achievement, they may even evaluate more favorably subordinates who do not bring problems to them.

Nevertheless, for the good of the organization, the boss, and the subordinate, a superior needs to hear about failures as well as successes. Some subordinates deal with a goodnews-only boss by finding indirect ways to get the necessary information to him or her, such as a management information system. Others see to it that potential problems, whether in the form of good surprises or bad news, are communicated immediately.

Dependability and Honesty. Few things are more disabling to a boss than a subordinate on whom he cannot depend, whose work he cannot trust. Almost no one is intentionally undependable, but many managers are inadvertently so because of oversight or uncertainty about the boss's priorities. A commitment to an optimistic delivery date may please a superior in the short term but become a source of displeasure if not honored. It's difficult for a boss to rely on a subordinate who repeatedly slips deadlines. As one president (describing a subordinate) put it: "I'd rather he be more consistent even if he delivered fewer peak successes at least I could rely on him."

Nor are many managers intentionally dishonest with their bosses. But it is easy to shade the truth and play down issues. Current concerns often become future surprise problems. It's almost impossible for bosses to work effectively if they cannot rely on a fairly accurate reading from their subordinates. Because it undermines credibility, dishonesty is perhaps the most troubling trait a subordinate can have. Without a basic level of trust, a boss feels compelled to check all of a subordinate's decisions, which makes it difficult to delegate.

Good Use of Time and Resources. Your boss is probably as limited in his or her store of time, energy, and influence as you are. Every request you make of your boss uses up some of these resources, so it's wise to draw on these resources selectively. This may sound obvious, but many managers use up their boss's time (and some of their own credibility) over relatively trivial issues.

One vice president went to great lengths to get his boss to fire a meddlesome secretary in another department. His boss had to use considerable influence to do it. Understandably, the head of the other department was not pleased. Later, when the vice president wanted to tackle more important problems, he ran into trouble. By using up blue chips on a relatively trivial issue, he had made it difficult for him and his boss to meet more important goals.

No doubt, some subordinates will resent that on top of all their other duties, they also need to take time and energy to manage their relationships with their bosses. Such managers fail to realize the importance of this activity and how it can simplify their jobs by eliminating potentially severe problems. Effective managers recognize that this part of their work is legitimate. Seeing themselves as ultimately responsible for what they achieve in an organization, they know they need to establish and manage relationships with everyone on whom they depend—and that includes the boss.

Checklist for Managing Your Boss

Make sure you understand your boss and his or her context, including:

- Goals and objectives

- Pressures

- Strengths, weaknesses, blind spots

- Preferred work style

Assess yourself and your needs, including:

- Strengths and weaknesses

- Personal style

- Predisposition toward dependence on authority figures

Develop and maintain a relationship that:

- Fits both your needs and styles

- Is characterized by mutual expectations

- Keeps your boss informed

- Is based on dependability and honesty

- Selectively uses your boss's time and resources

The Idea in Brief

Managing our *bosses* ? Isn't that merely manipulation? Corporate cozying up? Out-andout apple polishing? In fact, we manage our bosses for very good reasons: to get resources to do the best job, not only for ourselves, but for our bosses and our companies as well. We actively pursue a healthy and productive working relationship based on mutual respect and understanding—understanding our own and our bosses' strengths, weaknesses, goals, work styles, and needs. Here's what can happen when we don't:

Example: A new president with a formal work style replaced someone who'd been looser, more intuitive. The new president preferred written reports and structured meetings. One of his managers found this too controlling. He seldom sent background information, and was often blindsided by unanticipated questions. His boss found their meetings inefficient and frustrating. The manager had to resign.

In contrast, here's how another manager's sensitivity to this same boss's style really paid off:

Example: This manager identified the kinds and frequency of information the president wanted. He sent ahead background reports and discussion agendas. The result? Highly productive meetings and even more innovative problem solving than with his previous boss.

Managers often don't realize how much their bosses depend on them. They need cooperation, reliability, and honesty from their direct reports. Many managers also don't realize how much *they* depend on their bosses for links to the rest of the organization, for setting priorities, and for obtaining critical resources.

Recognizing this mutual dependence, effective managers seek out information about the boss's concerns and are sensitive to his work style. They also understand how their own attitudes toward authority can sabotage the relationship. Some see the boss as the enemy and fight him at every turn; others are overly compliant, viewing the boss as an all-wise parent.

You can benefit from this mutual dependence and develop a very productive relationship with your boss by focusing on compatible work styles. Bosses process information differently. "Listeners" prefer to be briefed in person so they can ask questions. "Readers" want to process written information first, and then meet to discuss.

Decision-making styles also vary. Some bosses are highly involved. Touch base with them frequently. Others prefer to delegate. Inform them about important decisions you've already made. mutual expectations. Don't passively assume you know what the boss expects. Find out. With some bosses, write detailed outlines of your work for their approval. With others, carefully planned discussions are key.

Also, communicate *your* expectations to find out if they are realistic. Persuade the boss to accept the most important ones, information flow. Managers typically underestimate what their bosses need to know and what they *do* know. Keep the boss informed through processes that fit his style.

Be forthright about both good and bad news dependability and honesty. Trustworthy subordinates only make promises they can keep and don't shade the truth or play down difficult issues, good use of time and resources. Don't waste your boss's time with trivial issues. Selectively draw on his time and resources to meet the most important goals—yours, his, and the company's.

CHAPTER 4

Be a Great Intimidators Leader

We hear a lot of praise for emotionally intelligent, even humble leaders. But change is scary, and you sometimes need scary leaders to steer you through. Those with bold political intelligence can creatively push followers to overperform. by Roderick M. Kramer

"Since when has being a difficult boss been a disqualifier for a job?" asked *Nightline*'s Ted Koppel after several abrasive, intimidating leaders of major corporations Disney's Michael Eisner, Miramax's Harvey Weinstein, and Hewlett-Packard's Carly Fiorina fell from their heights of power. Picking up on what seemed to be a new trend in the workplace, the business media quickly proclaimed that the reign of such leaders was over. From now on, the *Wall Street Journal* predicted, "tough guys will finish last."

But wait a minute, you might think. If they're just plain bad for their organizations, why have so many of these leaders made it to the top in the first place? Wouldn't the ones who've wreaked nothing but havoc have plateaued or been weeded out long before they could inflict too much damage? Yet many leaders who rule through intimidation have been doing just fine for a very long time. Before we proclaim their extinction, then, it's worth taking a close look at the pros as well as the cons of their tough-minded approach. Doing so might cast light on some subtle dimensions of effective leadership, especially in organizations or industries that were once rigid or unruly, stagnant or drifting places where it took an abrasive leader to shake things up a little and provide redirection.

Consider Ed Zander, who's been hailed as "Motorola's modernizer." When Zander took over as CEO of Motorola in January 2004, the company was in steep decline. After being in the high-velocity world of Silicon Valley, Zander found himself at the helm of a company that seemed to be running, in his words, "on autopilot." In taking on the challenge of turning Motorola around, Zander described his guiding philosophy as, "Whack yourself before somebody whacks you." He observed, "A lot of companies have clogged arteries." In Motorola's case, Zander found that much of the problem was at the VP level. "I don't know how many dozens of VPs are no longer with us," he reported in one interview. "Some have left on their own accord, some have not." The transformation at Motorola is far from com plete, but it is off to a good start. In the third quarter of 2004, the company posted sales of $8.62 billion (a 26% increase from the third quarter of 2003). Moreover, shipments of ist handsets were up 15% from the previous year.

A similar story can be told about Harvey Weinstein, also notorious for his abrasiveness. When he entered the Hollywood scene, a handful of major studios dominated the landscape. Independent picture producers limped along on the margins of power and influence. Weinstein almost single-handedly pulled the independent film industry out of the doldrums, in the process making Miramax one of the few widely recognized industry brand names. He didn't make a lot of friends over the years, and people who have worked with him often say that they find him hard to take. At the same time, they know that his high-pressure tactics have pushed them to the apex of their professional talents. One former Miramax executive noted appreciatively, "You learned to anticipate... the direction Harvey was going or wanted to go, because most of the time he was right." And there is no contending with Weinstein's success: more than 240 Academy Award nominations and 60 wins.

Zander and Weinstein are examples of what I call *great intimidators* . They are not averse to causing a ruckus, nor are they above using a few public whippings and ceremonial hangings to get attention. And they're in good company. A list of great intimidators would read a bit like a business leadership hall of fame: Sandy Weill, Rupert Murdoch, Andy Grove, Carly Fiorina, Larry Ellison, and Steve Jobs would be just a few of the names on it. These leaders seem to relish the chaos they create because, in their minds, it's constructive. Time is short, the stakes are high, and the measures required are draconian.

But make no mistake the great intimidators are not your typical bullies. If you're just a bully, it's all about humiliating others in an effort to make yourself feel good. Something very different is going on with the great intimidators. To be sure, they aren't above engaging in a little bullying to get their way. With them, however, the motivating factor isn't ego or gratuitous humiliation; it's vision. The great intimidators see a possible path through the thicket, and they're impatient to clear it. They chafe at impediments, even those that are human. They don't suffer from doubt or timidity. They've got a disdain for constraints imposed by others.

The modus operandi of great intimidators runs counter to a lot of our most deeply entrenched preconceptions about what it means to be a good leader these days. We've all read the books and articles describing people who lead quietly and with great empathy and humility. But as you'll see, the leaders I've been studying think and work in an entirely different way: They're rough, loud, and in your face.

Beneath their tough exteriors and sharp edges, however, are some genuine, deep insights into human motivation and organizational behavior. Indeed, these leaders possess what I call *political intelligence,* a distinctive and powerful form of leader intelligence that's been largely ignored by management theorists and practitioners. In all our recent enchantment with social intelligence and soft power, we've overlooked the kinds of skills leaders need to bring about transformation in cases of tremendous resistance or inertia. It's precisely in such situations, I'd like to propose, that the political intelligence of the intimidating leader is called for.

Political Intelligence at Work

What exactly is so special about political intelligence?

And how does it help set the great intimidators apart from other kinds of effective leaders? To answer these questions, we need to start by looking at conventional conceptions of leader intelligence.

Over the past decade, management theorists and practitioners alike have come to appreciate the roles that different forms of human intelligence play in effective leadership. Psychologist Howard Gardner who first articulated the theory of multiple intelligences suggested, for example, that social intelligence is what makes some leaders so adept at getting others to follow them and at extracting maximum performance from subordinates. Gardner defined social intelligence in terms of leaders' interpersonal skills, such as empathy and the ability to influence others on the basis of that understanding.

There's no question that it's important for all leaders to have these skills. Indeed, social intelligence is the sort of competency leaders rely on every day to accomplish the routine work of an organization. However, it's not the *only* kind of intelligence they need. What's more, in some settings (a rigidly hierarchical organiza tion, for example), other forms of intelligence may be more useful. That's when the application of political intelligence, the hallmark of great intimidators, can make the difference between paralysis and successful if sometimes wrenching—organizational change.

In understanding the distinction between socially intelligent and politically intelligent leaders, it's important to realize that they share certain skills. Both types of leaders are adept at sizing up other people. Both possess keen, discriminating eyes—but they notice different things. For instance, socially intelligent leaders assess people's strengths and figure out how to leverage them, while politically intelligent leaders focus on people's weaknesses and insecurities. Speaking of President Lyndon B. Johnson, one of history's truly great intimidators, former press secretary Bill Moyers noted that he possessed "an animal sense of weakness in other men."As one political scientist elaborated, Johnson "studied, analyzed, catalogued, and remembered the strengths and weaknesses, the likes and dislikes, of fellow politicians as some men do stock prices, batting averages, and musical compositions. He knew who drank Scotch and who bourbon, whose wife was sick…who was in trouble and who owed him."

Not only do socially intelligent and politically intelligent leaders notice different things; they also *act* differently on the basis of their divergent perceptions. While leaders with social intelligence use empathy and soft power to build bridges, politically intelligent leaders use intimidation and hard power to exploit the anxieties and vulnerabilities they detect. Both kinds of leaders are good judges of character. But instead of having empathy for others, the politically intelligent leader adopts a dispassionate, clinical, even instrumental view of people as resources for getting things done. This absence of empathy opens up branches of the decision tree, exposing options that other leaders might reject.

Perhaps the starkest point of contrast between these two kinds of leaders is how willing they are to use hard power. Politically intelligent leaders appreciate the power of fear and its close relation, anxiety. As Harvard University's president, Larry Summers, once observed: "Sometimes fear does the work of reason." He went to Harvard determined to shake up the institution and whatever else may be said about him, he has succeeded in doing just that. Interviews with faculty, staff, and students at Harvard who've had close encounters with Summers reveal a common pattern in his interactions: initial confrontation, followed by skeptical and hard questioning. "Perhaps we don't really even need a department like this at Harvard," he is said to have told one group of faculty at a "let's get acquainted" session.

Such questions may not make a leader popular, but they certainly wake people up. And they sometimes compel people to think more deeply about their purpose in an organization and the value they add to it. In asking them to justify their existence, for instance, Summers has forced professors and administrators at Harvard to become more thoughtful about what they do. So though it can be painful, that exercise in justification leads to greater clarity about purpose and strategy. As Harvard Law School professor Alan Dershowitz bluntly pointed out in a television interview, "Most [university] presidents are too careful, too cautious, too frightened, too worried about tipping the boat, too worried about alienating anybody, too worried about offending anybody." Dershowitz went on to add that Summers" *is* a provocative president. I think in my 41 years at Harvard I have never seen a more exciting time, more diversity of views…and I think Harvard is a better place for it."

Summers's sentiments regarding the virtues of inculcating a little fear echo one of President Richard Nixon's convictions: "People react to fear, not love they don't teach that in Sunday school, but it's true." For Nixon, leadership wasn't about inspiring others or being liked; it was about producing tangible results. And although too much fear or anxiety may induce trepidation and paralysis, too little may result in lackluster effort and complacency.

The great intimidators force people to review how strongly they feel about an issue. Are they really willing to go to the mat for it? If so, then they had better have a strong argument. It's then that the debate gets interesting, both for the individuals involved and for the organization. One Microsoft manager told me, "Bill Gates relishes intellectual combat. He hires the best and brightest and most articulate individuals because he wants the conversation to be at the highest possible level."

The Intimidator's Tactics

When it comes to understanding how politically intelligent leaders achieve such stunning results, the devil is in the details, and the details are to be found in the effective but sometimes extreme tactics these leaders use to coerce their subordinates to overperform.

Get up close and personal.

Many intimidators operate through direct confrontation. At times, they will even invade the personal space of the people they want to control. This mode of intimidation fits our stereotype of the hulking organizational bully. Universal Pictures chair Stacey Snider found herself on the receiving end of this sort of treatment during an unexpected confrontation with Miramax's Harvey Weinstein at a cocktail party. Weinstein was upset because of rumors circulating throughout Hollywood that he had started a whispering campaign to discredit Universal's film *A Beautiful Mind* . At a celebratory dinner following the Golden Globes, at which *A Beautiful Mind* won several awards, including best drama, Weinstein cornered Snider. In a *New Yorker* article, Ken Auletta described their close encounter this way: "To the petite Snider, [Weinstein] was a fearsome sight his eyes dark and glowering, his fleshy face unshaved, his belly jutting forward half a foot or so ahead of his body. He jabbed a finger at Snider's face and screamed, 'You're going to go down for this!'" This was the calculated sound and fury of a skillful intimidator. Snider understood that, and she held her ground with Weinstein.

A sure sign of the extent to which truly great intimidators are putting on an act is the fact that many of them work on their tactics when alone. General George Patton used to practice his scowl in front of his mirror. He called it his "general's face," and he wanted it to be as terrifying and menacing a countenance as he could make it. Entrepreneur Reggie Lewis also admitted that he spent time in front of his mirror perfecting what became his trademark frown. He believed that to really excel at hardball, it helped to have a face that fit the part.

In addition to aggressive physical demeanors, intimidators routinely use the weapons of language—taunts and slurs—to provoke their victims. This behavior is designed to throw others off balance. It's hard to think clearly and follow your own game plan when your buttons are being pushed. Clarence Thomas, associate justice of the U.S. Supreme Court, used this tactic to browbeat his Democratic opponents on the Senate judiciary committee during his nomination hearings. When accused by Anita Hill of sexual harassment, he asked the members of the committee how they would like to be so accused. The discomfort of the committee (which included an understandably subdued Ted Kennedy) was palpable. To complete the trick, he threw the race card down on the table, calling the procedure "a high-tech lynching for uppity blacks who in any way deign to think for themselves...[and don't] kowtow to an old order." By putting the committee on the defensive, Thomas pulled the moral high ground right out from under their feet.

Be angry.

Most intimidators use anger and rage to get their way. A calculated "loss of temper" does more than help intimidators prevail in the heat of the moment, though. It also serves as a chilling deterrent for potential challengers. While in some instances they are clearly putting on an act, intimidators aren't always in full control of their emotions when they go off on tirades. But even then a loss of control can be useful. As political pundit Chris Matthews once said, "Don't have a reputation for being a nice guy that won't do you any good." He cited his experience working with former Maine senator Ed Muskie: "Muskie was the best of them all, the absolute best, because nobody wanted to tangle with the guy. You know, why tangle with the guy? Why ruin your day? A bad temper is a very powerful political tool because most people don't like confrontation." People will think twice before confronting you if you've got a reputation for being willing to scorch a little earth rather than back down.

This point may seem simple and obvious, but it's worth emphasizing because people often don't fully appreciate how much ground they may yield simply to keep intimidating leaders from getting in their face or ruining their day. Without consciously or completely realizing it, they may even leave the playing field in order to avoid an unpleasant encounter. Or they may hold back in the hope that someone else will stand up to the great intimidator.

Either way, intimidators end up getting what they want. Contrived anger of this type is especially prevalent among politicians. Indeed, Pulitzer-winning journalist Hedrick Smith has even given a name to it: porcupine power.

Keep them guessing.

Many leadership books these days tout the importance of transparency. We trust leaders when we feel we know their intentions and motives, a lot of authors say. According to this view, leaders must take great pains to be sure other people understand them and why they are doing what they're doing. Intimidators don't buy into this idea at all. They prefer to remain unfathomable because this keeps subordinates on their toes and makes it easier to change direction without losing credibility. If people don't know where you're coming from or where you're going, it's easier to catch them by surprise.

Some leaders preserve their mystery through deliberate distance; many of the great intimidators I've studied cultivated an aloof demeanor with subordinates. When he was U.S. Secretary of Defense, Robert McNamara was especially famous for his cold and distant style. As journalist and historian David Halberstam noted in *The Reckoning*, "He shunned small talk. Small talk wasted time and encouraged intimacies. Intimacies were unwanted, at least with employees." McNamara's intimidating demeanor with subordinates and rivals *was* an act. He had no trouble turning on the charm with those he wanted to please. With presidents Kennedy and Johnson—the men he had chosen to serve—he was uniformly described as warm, witty, and attentive. He was such an interesting and pleasant conversationalist that his presence was enthusiastically sought at Washington cocktail parties. As McNamara's behavior illustrates, great intimidators can also be great ingratiators and seem to be able to change their demeanor in a chameleon-like way to suit their needs.

Silence and sullenness are also powerful tools. "You're not sure why the person is displeased with you, but you sure sense it," one former HP employee told me when describing a meeting she'd had with Carly Fiorina. Subordinates of silent, sullen intimidators end up spending a lot of time huddled around the watercooler trying to figure out whether they're in or out and then go and sit in their offices and dream up ways of pleasing the boss. The really skillful silent intimidators even make it hard for followers to know for certain that they are even intimidating you. If confronted about their behavior, they are likely to protest innocence, claiming you've got them all wrong: "Who, me? You're just being paranoid!" Many subordinates have accused Disney's Eisner of this kind of behavior.

Know it all.

Mastery of the facts or at least the appearance of it—can also be hugely intimidating. "Informational intimidators" always have facts and figures at their fingertips, while their opponents are still trying to formulate an argument or retrieve something from memory. British prime minister Margaret Thatcher was legendary for her ability to silence or paralyze her opponents with her superior command of whatever topic was being debated. As one observer noted, Thatcher was a "demon for information, for research, for numbers. She devoured them, [and] she remembered them…No one could out-study or out-prepare her." In one famous confrontation in the House of Commons, Thatcher took on and "battered into submission" the able and respected Richard Crossman. "It was obvious," recalled John Boyd-Carpenter, the cabinet minister in charge at the time. "She had done her homework, and he had not done his." Often, it doesn't even matter all that much whether the "facts" are right.

When it comes to making a good impression or anchoring an argument, the truly great intimidator seizes the advantage. Even the misleading or inaccurate factoid when uttered with complete confidence and injected into a discussion with perfect timing and precision can carry the day. In a negotiation or board meeting, less confident individuals are likely to remain silent and avoid challenging someone presenting her case with assurance. It's only later, when there might be time to check out the accuracy of a statement, that people realize they've been hoodwinked. By then, however, it's too late: The moment is gone, and the informational intimidator has walked away with all the marbles. Robert McNamara raised this technique to the level of an art. When he and Lee Iacocca were at Ford, Iacocca once commented to another executive, "That son of a bitch [McNamara] always has an answer, and it always sounds good. But you know," he added, "I checked some of it out after a meeting, and some of it is really bullshit. Stuff he just made up."

The Intimidator's Magnetism

At this point, you might be wondering just what the draw is. Great intimidators trample on people's feelings and set impossible standards. Even when others meet those standards, they're given little if any credit.

But despite all the drawbacks, my research shows, great intimidators are often magnets for the best and brightest. Consider the brilliant Nobelist James Watson, one of the scientists who discovered the helical structure of DNA. Edward O. Wilson, the famous Harvard sociobiologist, recounted what it was like to be a colleague of Watson's: "He arrived with such a conviction that biology must be transformed....[He felt that] what had gone before was infested by stamp collectors who lacked the wit to transform their subject into a modern science." Wilson continued, "At department meetings Watson radiated contempt in all directions. He shunned ordinary courtesy and polite conversation, evidently in the belief that they would encourage the traditionalists to stay around...[and he spoke] with casual and brutal offhandedness." Not surprisingly, few dared call Watson on the carpet. But Watson's students many of whom achieved their own eminence pointed out that he was inspiring as well as demanding. As one put it, Watson "always introduced the right mixture of fear and paranoia so that we worked our asses off."

There are many such stories in business. A former executive of Martha Stewart's told me what it was like to work with Stewart on a project: She had the most amazingly well-organized and disciplined mind I've ever known. She grasped things instantly, and she had the ability to direct your attention to the single most important thing you should be thinking about or doing at that particular moment. She could be incredibly impatient and brusque if you were slow on the uptake but if you could keep up with her, and perform to her standard, it was tremendously satisfying.

A former Apple executive who had been involved with the launch of the original Macintosh computer in 1984 had similar things to say about Steve Jobs: "[He] was the most difficult human being I've ever worked for but he was also the most technologically brilliant. No one knew technology better than he did, and no one had a clearer sense of where it was going."

Intimidators instill fear in their employees, but the really great ones instill something else as well and that's another way in which they are different from your run-of-the-mill organizational bully. As one former aide of legendary tough guy Admiral Hyman Rickover told me, "Not measuring up in his eyes meant more to me than anything else even my father's." In a similar vein, a former Pixar employee said of his time working under Steve Jobs, "You just dreaded letting him down. He believed in you so strongly that the thought of disappointing him just killed you."

As these quotes make clear, people like to work for great intimidators because of what can be learned from them and because they inspire great performance. Many of the people I spoke with said they did their best work ever when working for a great intimidator. But the appeal goes beyond that. A lot of people are fascinated by difficult leaders because they want to possess a little "inner intimidator" of their own. During a senior executive education program on power and leadership that I teach every year at Stanford University, I once asked participants to indicate which leadership qualities they felt they most lacked and which ones they wished they possessed more of. I fully expected them to cite the sorts of qualities associated with social and emotional intelligence, celebrated by Daniel Goleman and others. Yet, surprisingly, a large number of these accomplished executives named attributes like toughness and forcefulness. Despite their proven success, these leaders felt they were still *too nice* and too concerned about what their employees thought of them.

All the program participants considered themselves strong on people skills they generally thought they had social intelligence in abundance and knew how to wield soft power to great effect. Yet they felt that their socially intelligent selves sometimes got in the way of their ability to do the dirty work needed to raise their organizations to the next level of performance. Being sufficiently tough, they seemed to sense, required something that didn't come so naturally or easily to them (and perhaps to most of us). One executive, for instance, told me that he yearned to possess more of a command presence when dealing with his board. Another said, "I would love to have Carly [Fiorina]'s ability to stare down her opponents." The participants felt that they had achieved less than they might have, and they attributed the shortfall in performance to their failure to fully and effectively use their positional power. To put it another way, they believed that they could stand to be a little less socially intelligent and a little more politically intelligent.

The Idea in Brief

When it comes to understanding how politically intelligent leaders achieve such stunning results, the devil is in the details, and the details are to be found in the effective but sometimes extreme tactics these leaders use to coerce their subordinates to overperform.

Get up close and personal. Many intimidators operate through direct confrontation. At times, they will even invade the personal space of the people they want to control. This mode of intimidation fits our stereotype of the hulking organizational bully.

Be angry. Most intimidators use anger and rage to get their way. A calculated "loss of temper" does more than help intimidators prevail in the heat of the moment, though. It also serves as a chilling deterrent for potential challengers. While in some instances they are clearly putting on an act, intimidators aren't always in full control of their emotions when they go off on tirades. But even then a loss of control can be useful.

Keep them guessing. Many leadership books these days tout the importance of transparency. We trust leaders when we feel we know their intentions and motives, a lot of authors say. According to this view, leaders must take great pains to be sure other people understand them and why they are doing what they're doing. Intimidators don't buy into this idea at all. They prefer to remain unfathomable because this keeps subordinates on their toes and makes it easier to change direction without losing credibility.

Know it all. Mastery of the facts or at least the appearance of it—can also be hugely intimidating. "Informational intimidators" always have facts and figures at their fingertips, while their opponents are still trying to formulate an argument or retrieve something from memory.

CHAPTER 5

Interpersonal Barriers to Decision Making

The actual behavior of top executives during decision-making meetings often does not jibe with their attitudes and prescriptions about effective executive action.

The gap that often exists between what executives say and how they behave helps create barriers to openness and trust, to the effective search for alternatives, to innovation, and to flexibility in the organization.

These barriers are more destructive in important decision-making meetings than in routine meetings, and they upset effective managers more than ineffective ones. The barriers cannot be broken down simply by intellectual exercises. Rather, executives need feedback concerning their behavior and opportunities to develop self-awareness in action. To this end, certain kinds of questioning are valuable; playing back and analyzing tape recordings of meetings has proved to be a helpful step; and laboratory education programs are valuable.

These are a few of the major findings of a study of executive decision making in six representative companies. The findings have vital implications for management groups everywhere; for while some organizations are less subject to the weaknesses described than are others, *all* groups have them in some degree. In this article I shall discuss the findings in detail and examine the implications for executives up and down the line.

Words vs. Actions

According to top management, the effectiveness of decision-making activities depends on the degree of innovation, risk taking, flexibility, and trust in the executive system. (Risk taking is defined here as any act where the executive risks his self-esteem. This could be a moment, for example, when he goes against the group view; when he tells someone, especially the person with the highest power, something negative about his impact on the organization; or when he seeks to put millions of dollars in a new investment.)

Nearly 95% of the executives in our study emphasize that an organization is only as good as its top people. They constantly repeat the importance of their responsibility to help themselves and others to develop their abilities. Almost as often they report that the qualities just mentioned—motivation, risk taking, and so on—are key characteristics of any successful executive system. "People problems" head the list as the most difficult, perplexing, and crucial.

In short, the executives vote overwhelmingly for executive systems where the contributions of each executive can be maximized and where innovation, risk taking, flexibility, and trust reign supreme. Nevertheless, the *behavior* of these same executives tends to create decision-making processes that are *not* very effective. Their behavior can be fitted into two basic patterns:

Pattern A—thoughtful, rational, and mildly competitive. This is the behavior most frequently observed during the decision-making meetings. Executives following this pattern own up to their ideas in a style that emphasizes a serious concern for ideas. As they constantly battle for scarce resources and "sell" their views, their openness to others' ideas is relatively high, not because of a sincere interest in learning about the point of view of others, but so they can engage in a form of "one-upmanship"— that is, gain information about the others' points of view in order to politely discredit them.

Pattern B—competitive first, thoughtful and rational second. In this pattern, conformity to ideas replaces concern for ideas as the strongest norm. Also, antagonism to ideas is higher—in many cases higher than openness to ideas. The relatively high antagonism scores usually indicate, in addition to high competitiveness, a high degree of conflict and pent-up feelings, helping others to own up, be open, and take risks; using a style of behavior that supports the norm of individuality and trust as well as mistrust; expressing feelings, positive or negative.

EXHIBIT I summarizes data for four illustrative groups of managers—two groups with Pattern A characteristics and two with Pattern B characteristics.

These results should not be interpreted as implying that the executives do not have feelings. We know from the interviews that many of the executives have strong feelings indeed. However, the overwhelming majority (84%) feel that it is a sign of immaturity to express feelings openly *during decision-making meetings.* Nor should the results be interpreted to mean that the executives do not enjoy risk taking. The data permit us to conclude only that few risk-taking actions were *observed* during the meetings. (Also, we have to keep in mind that the executives were always observed in groups; it may be that their behavior in groups varies significantly from their behavior as individuals.)

Before I attempt to give my views about the reasons for the discrepancy between executives' words and actions, I should like to point out that these results are not unique to business organizations. I have obtained similar behavior patterns from leaders in education, research, the ministry, trade unions, and government. Indeed, one of the fascinating questions for me is why so many different people in so many different kinds of organizations tend to manifest similar problems.

Exhibit I. Management Groups with Pattern A and Pattern B Characteristics

	PATTERN A				PATTERN B			
	GROUP 1		GROUP 2		GROUP 3		GROUP 4	
TOTAL NUMBER OF UNITS ANALYZED*	198		143		201		131	
UNITS CHARACTERIZED BY:	NUMBER	PERCENT	NUMBER	PERCENT	NUMBER	PERCENT	NUMBER	PERCENT
OWNING UP TO OWN IDEAS	146	74	105	74	156	78	102	78
CONCERN FOR OTHERS' IDEAS	122	62	89	62	52	26	56	43
CONFORMITY TO OTHERS' IDEAS	54	27	38	26	87	43	62	47
OPENNESS TO OTHERS' IDEAS	46	23	34	24	31	15	25	19
INDIVIDUALITY	4	2	12	8	30	15	8	6
ANTAGONISM TO OTHERS' IDEAS	18	9	4	3	32	16	5	4
UNWILLINGNESS TO HELP OTHERS OWN UP TO THEIR IDEAS	5	2	3	2	14	7	4	3

* A unit is an instance of a manager speaking on a topic. If during the course of speaking he changes to a new topic, another unit is created.

Why the Discrepancy?

The more I observe such problems in different organizations possessing different technologies and varying greatly in size, the more I become impressed with the importance of the role played by the values or assumptions top people hold on the nature of effective human relationships and the best ways to run an organization.

Basic values

In the studies so far I have isolated three basic values that seem to be very important:

1. *The significant human relationships are the ones which have to do with achieving the organization's objective.* My studies of over 265 different types and sizes of meetings indicate that executives almost always tend to focus their behavior on "getting the job done." In literally thousands of units of behavior, almost none are observed where the men spend some time in analyzing and maintaining their group's effectiveness. This is true even though in many meetings the group's effectiveness "bogged down" and the objectives were not being reached because of interpersonal factors. When the executives are interviewed and asked why they did not spend some time in examining the group opera tions or processes, they reply that they were there to get a job done. They add: "If the group isn't effective, it is up to the leader to get it back on the track by directing it."

2. *Cognitive rationality is to be emphasized; feelings and emotions are to be played down.* This value influences executives to see cognitive, intellectual discussions as "relevant," "good," "work," and so on. Emotional and interpersonal discussions tend to be viewed as "irrelevant," "immature," "not work," and so on. As a result, when emotions and interpersonal variables become blocks to group effectiveness, all the executives report feeling that they should *not* deal with them. For example, in the event of an emotional disagreement, they would tell the members to "get back to facts" or "keep personalities out of this."

3. *Human relationships are most effectively influenced through unilateral direction, coercion, and control, as well as by rewards and penalties that sanction all three values.* This third value of direction and control is implicit in the chain of command and also in the elaborate managerial controls that have been developed within organizations.

Influence on operations

The impact of these values can be considerable. For example, to the extent that individuals dedicate themselves to the value of intellectual rationality and "getting the job done," they will tend to be aware of and emphasize the intellectual aspects of issues in an organization and (consciously or unconsciously) to suppress the interpersonal and emotional aspects, especially those which do not seem relevant to achieving the task.

As the interpersonal and emotional aspects of behavior become suppressed, organizational norms that coerce individuals to hide their feelings or to disguise them and bring them up as technical, intellectual problems will tend to arise.

Under these conditions the individual may tend to find it very difficult to develop competence in dealing with feelings and interpersonal relationships. Also, in a world where the expression of feelings is not valued, individuals may build personal and organizational defenses to help them suppress their own feelings or inhibit others in such expression. Or they may refuse to consider ideas which, if explored, could expose suppressed feelings.

Such a defensive reaction in an organization could eventually inhibit creativity and innovation during decision making. The participants might learn to limit themselves to those ideas and values that were not threatening. They might also decrease their openness to new ideas and values. And as the degree of openness decreased, the capacity to experiment would also decrease, and fear of taking risks would increase. This would reduce the *probability* of experimentation, thus decreasing openness to new ideas still further and constricting risk taking even more than formerly. We would thereby have a closed circuit which could become an important cause of loss of vitality in an organization.

Some Consequences

Aside from the impact of values on vitality, what are some other consequences of the executive behavior patterns earlier described on top management decision making and on the effective functioning of the organization? For the sake of brevity, I shall include only examples of those consequences that were found to exist in one form or another in all organizations studied.

Restricted commitment

One of the most frequent findings is that in major decisions that are introduced by the president, there tends to be less than open discussion of the issues, and the commitment of the officers tends to be less than complete (although they may assure the president to the contrary). For instance, consider what happened in one organization where a major administrative decision made during the period of the research was the establishment of several top management committees to explore basic long-range problems:

As is customary with major decisions, the president discussed it in advance at a meeting of the executive committee. He began the meeting by circulating, as a basis for discussion, a draft of the announcement of the committees. Most of the members' discussion was concerned with raising questions about the wording of the proposal:

- "Is the word *action* too strong?"
- "I recommend that we change 'steps can be taken' to 'recommendations can be made.' "
- "We'd better change the word 'lead' to 'maintain.' "

As the discussion seemed to come to an end, one executive said he was worried that the announcement of the committees might be interpreted by the people below as an implication "that the executive committee believes the organization is in trouble. Let's get the idea in that all is well." There was spontaneous agreement by all executives: "Hear, hear!"

A brief silence was broken by another executive who apparently was not satisfied with the concept of the committees. He raised a series of questions. The manner in which it was done was interesting. As he raised each issue, he kept assuring the president and the group that he was not against the concept. He just wanted to be certain that the executive committee was clear on what it was doing. For example, he assured them:

- "I'm not clear. Just asking."
- "I'm trying to get a better picture."
- "I'm just trying to get clarification."
- "Just so that we understand what the words mean."

The president nodded in agreement, but he seemed to become slightly impatient. He remarked that many of these problems would not arise if the members of these new committees took an overall company point of view. An executive commented (laughingly), "Oh, I'm for motherhood too!"

The proposal was tabled in order for the written statement to be revised and discussed further during the next meeting. It appeared that the proposal was the president's personal "baby," and the executive committee members would naturally go along with it. The most responsibility some felt was that they should raise questions so the president would be clear about *his* (not *their*) decision.

At the next meeting the decision-making process was the same as at the first. The president circulated copies of the revised proposal. During this session a smaller number of executives asked questions. Two pushed (with appropriate care) the notion that the duties of one of the committees were defined too broadly.

The president began to defend his proposal by citing an extremely long list of examples, indicating that in his mind "reasonable" people should find the duties clear. This comment and the long list of examples may have communicated to others a feeling that the president was becoming impatient. When he finished, there was a lengthy silence. The president then turned to one of the executives and asked directly, "Why are you worried about this?" The executive explained, then quickly added that as far as he could see the differences were not major ones and his point of view could be integrated with the president's by "changing some words."

The president agreed to the changes, looked up, and asked, "I take it now there is common agreement?" All executives replied "yes" or nodded their heads affirmatively.

As I listened, I had begun to wonder about the commitment of the executive committee members to the idea. In subsequent interviews I asked each about his view of the proposal. Half felt that it was a good proposal. The other half had reservations ranging from moderate to serious. However, being loyal members, they would certainly do their best to make it work, they said.

Subordinate gamesmanship

I can best illustrate the second consequence by citing from a study of the effectiveness of product planning and program review activities in another of the organizations studied:

I can best illustrate the second consequence by citing from a study of the effectiveness of product planning and program review activities in another of the organizations studied:

It was company policy that peers at any given level should make the decisions. Whenever they could not agree or whenever a decision went beyond their authority, the problem was supposed to be sent to the next higher level. The buck passing stopped at the highest level. A meeting with the president became a great event. Beforehand a group would "dry run" its presentation until all were satisfied that they could present their view effectively.

Few difficulties were observed when the meeting was held to present a recommendation agreed to by all at the lower levels. The difficulties arose when "negative" information had to be fed upward. For example, a major error in the program, a major delay, or a major disagreement among the members was likely to cause such trouble.

The dynamics of these meetings was very interesting. In one case the problem to present was a major delay in a development project. In the dry run the subordinates planned to begin the session with information that "updated" the president. The information was usually presented in such a way that slowly and carefully the president was alerted to the fact that a major problem was about to be announced. One could hear such key phrases as:

- "We are a bit later than expected."

- "We're not on plan."

- "We have had greater difficulties than expected."

- "It is now clear that no one should have promised what we did."

These phrases were usually followed by some reassuring statement such as:

- "However, we're on top of this."

- "Things are really looking better now."

- "Although we are late, we have advanced the state of the art."

- "If you give us another three months, we are certain that we can solve this problem."

To the observer's eyes, it is difficult to see how the president could deny the request. Apparently he felt the same way because he granted it. However, he took nearly 20 minutes to say that this shocked him; he was wondering if everyone was *really* doing everything they could; this was a serious program; this was not the way he wanted to see things run; he was sure they would agree with him; and he wanted their assurances that this would be the final delay.

A careful listening to the tape after the meeting brought out the fact that no subordinate gave such assurances. They simply kept saying that they were doing their best; they had poured a lot into this; or they had the best technical know-how working on it.

Another interesting observation is that most subordinates in this company, especially in presentations to the president, tended to go along with certain unwritten rules:

1. Before you give any bad news, give good news. Especially emphasize the capacity of the department to work hard and to rebound from a failure.

2. Play down the impact of a failure by emphasizing how close you came to achieving the target or how soon the target can be reached. If neither seems reasonable, emphasize how difficult it is to define such targets, and point out that because the state of the art is so primitive, the original commitment was not a wise one.

3. In a meeting with the president it is unfair to take advantage of another department that is in trouble, even if it is a "natural enemy." The sporting thing to do is say something nice about the other department and offer to help it in any way possible. (The offer is usually not made in concrete form, nor does the department in difficulty respond with the famous phrase, "What do you have in mind?")

The subordinates also were in agreement that too much time was spent in long presentations in order to make the president happy. The president, however, confided to the researcher that he did not enjoy listening to long and, at times, dry presentations (especially when he had seen most of the key data anyway). However, he felt that it was important to go through this because it might give the subordinates a greater sense of commitment to the problem!

Lack of awareness

One of our most common observations in company studies is that executives lack awareness of their own behavioral patterns as well as of the negative impact of their behavior on others. This is not to imply that they are completely unaware; each individual usually senses some aspects of a problem. However, we rarely find an individual or group of individuals who is aware of enough of the scope and depth of a problem so that the need for effective action can be fully understood.

For example, during the study of the decision-making processes of the president and the 9 vice presidents of a firm with nearly 3,000 employees, I concluded that the members unknowingly behaved in such a way as *not* to encourage risk taking, openness, expression of feelings, and cohesive, trusting relationships. But subsequent interviews with the 10 top executives showed that they held a completely different point of view from mine. They admitted that negative feelings were not expressed, but said the reason was that "we trust each other and respect each other." According to 6 of the men, individuality was high and conformity low; where conformity was agreed to be high, the reason given was the necessity of agreeing with the man who is boss. According to 8 of the men, "We help each other all the time." Issues loaded with conflict were not handled during meetings, it was reported, for these reasons:

- "We should not discuss emotional disagreements before the executive committee because when people are emotional, they are not rational."

- "We should not air our dirty linen in front of the people who may come in to make a presentation."

- "Why take up people's time with subjective debates?"

- "Most members are not acquainted with all the details. Under our system the person who presents the issues has really thought them through."

- "Pre-discussion of issues helps to prevent anyone from sandbagging the executive committee."

- "Rarely emotional; when it does happen, you can pardon it."

The executive committee climate or emotional tone was characterized by such words as:

- "Friendly."
- "Not critical of each other."
- M "Not tense."
- "Frank and no tensions because we've known each other for years."

How was I to fit the executives' views with mine? I went back and listened to all the interviews again. As I analyzed the tapes, I began to realize that an interesting set of contradictions arose during many of the interviews. In the early stages of the interviews the executives tended to say things that they contradicted later; EXHIBIT II contains examples of contradictions repeated by 6 or more of the 10 top executives.

EXHIBIT II. Contradictory Statements

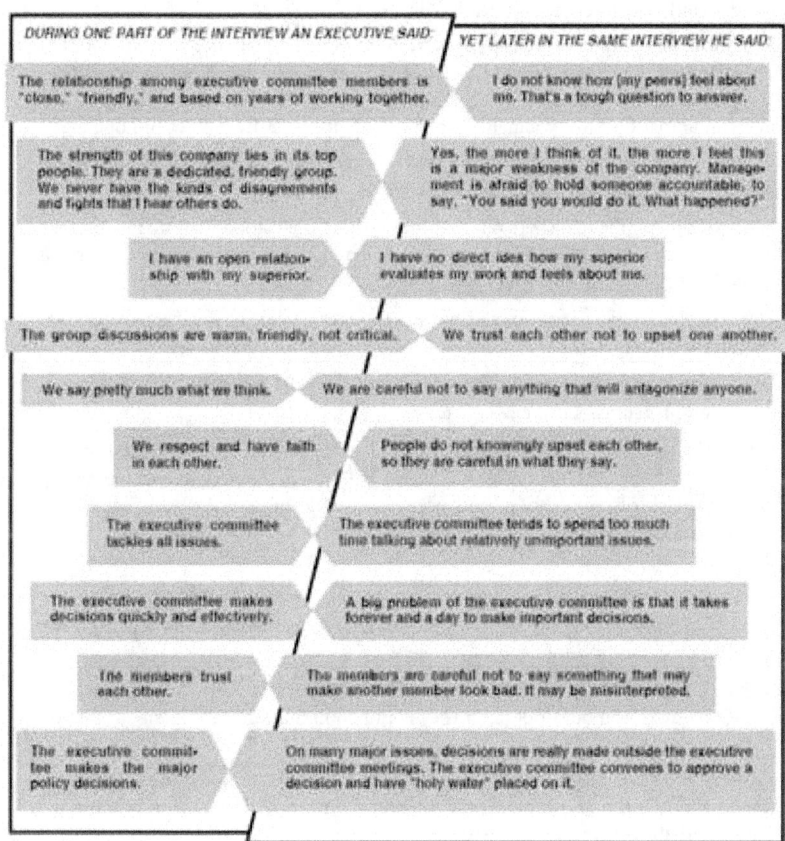

What accounts for these contradictions? My explanation is that over time the executives had come to mirror, in their behavior, the values of their culture (e.g., be rational, nonemotional, diplomatically open, and so on). They had created a culture that reinforced their own leadership styles. If an executive wanted to behave differently, he probably ran the risk of being considered a deviant. In most of the cases the executives decided to forgo this risk, and they behaved like the majority. These men, in order to live with themselves, probably had to develop various defenses and blinders about their acquiescence to an executive culture that may not have been the one they personally preferred and valued.

Incidentally, in this group there were two men who had decided to take the other route. Both men were viewed by the others as "a bit rough at the edges" or "a little too aggressive."

To check the validity of some of the findings reported, we interviewed the top 25 executives below the executive committee. If our analysis was correct, we knew, then they should tend to report that the members of the executive committee were low in openness to uncomfortable information, risk taking, trust, and capacity to deal with conflicts openly, and high in conformity. The results were as predicted (see EXHIBIT III).

Blind spots

Another result found in all organizations studied is the tendency for executives to be unaware of the negative feelings that their subordinates have about them. This finding is not startling in view of the fact that the executive problem-solving processes do not tend to reward the upward communication of information about interpersonal issues that is emotionally laden and risky to communicate. To illustrate:

In one organization, all but one of the top executive committee members reported that their relationships with their subordinates were "relatively good to excellent." When asked how they judged their relationships, most of the executives responded with such statements as: "They do everything that I ask for willingly," and "We talk together frequently and openly."

The picture from the middle management men who were the immediate subordinates was different. Apparently, top management was unaware that:

- 71% of the middle managers did not know where they stood with their superiors; they considered their relationships as ambiguous, and they were not aware of such important facts as how they were being evaluated.

- 65% of the middle managers did not know what qualities led to success in their organizations.

- 87% felt that conflicts were very seldom coped with; and that when they were, the attempts tended to be inadequate.

- 65% thought that the most important unsolved problem of the organization was that the top management was unable to help them overcome the intergroup rivalries, lack of cooperation, and poor communications; 53% said that if they could alter one aspect of their superior's behavior, it would be to help him see the "dog eat dog" communication problems that existed in middle management.

- 59% evaluated top management effectiveness as not too good or about average; and 62% reported that the development of a cohesive management team was the second most important unsolved problem.

- 82% of the middle managers wished that the status of their function and job could be increased but doubted if they could communicate this openly to the top management.

Interestingly, in all the cases that I have observed where the president asked for a discussion of any problems that the top and middle management men present thought important, the problems mentioned above were never raised.

Rather, the most frequently mentioned problem (74% of the cases) was the overload problem. The executives and managers reported that they were overloaded and that the situation was getting worse. The president's usual reply was that he appreciated their predicament, but "that is life." The few times he asked if the men had any suggestions, he received such replies as "more help," "fewer meetings," "fewer reports," "delay of schedules," and so on. As we will see, few of these suggestions made sense, since the men were asking either for increases in costs or for a decrease in the very controls that the top management used to administer the organization.

EXHIBIT III.   How the Executive Committee Was Rated by 25
Executives Below It

NUMBER OF MANAGERS RATING THE COMMITTEE AS:

CHARACTERISTIC RATED	LOW	MODERATE	HIGH
OPENNESS TO UNCOMFORTABLE INFORMATION*	12	6	4
RISK TAKING	20	4	1
TRUST	14	9	2
CONFORMITY	0	2	23
ABILITY TO DEAL WITH CONFLICTS	19	6	0

*Three executives gave a "don't know" response.

Distrust & antagonism

Another result of the behavior patterns earlier described is that management tends to keep promotions semisecret and most of the actual reasons for executive changes completely secret. Here is an example from an organization whose board we studied in some detail over a period of two years:

The executives complained of three practices of the board about which the board members were apparently unaware: (1) the constant alteration of organizational positions and charts, and keeping the most up-to-date versions semiconfidential; (2) shifting top executives without adequate discussion with all executives involved and without clearly communicating the real reasons for the move; and (3) developing new departments with product goals that overlapped and competed with the goals of already existing departments.

The board members admitted these practices but tended not to see them as being incompatible with the interests of the organization. For example, to take the first complaint, they defended their practice with such statements as: "If you tell them everything, all they do is worry, and we get a flood of rumors"; "The changes do not *really* affect them"; and, "It will only cut in on their busy schedule and interrupt their productivity."

The void of clear-cut information from the board was, however, filled in by the executives. Their explanations ranged from such statements as "They must be changing things because they are not happy with the way things are going" to "The unhappiness is so strong they do not tell us." Even the executives who profited from some of these moves reported some concern and bewilderment. For example, three reported instances where they had been promoted over some "old-timers." In all cases they were told to "soft-pedal the promotion aspect" until the oldtimers were diplomatically informed. Unfortunately, it took months to inform the latter men, and in some cases it was never done.

There was another practice of the board that produced difficulties in the organization:

Department heads cited the board's increasing intervention into the detailed administration of a department when its profit picture looked shaky. This practice was, from these subordinates' view, in violation of the stated philosophy of decentralization.

When asked, board members tended to explain this practice by saying that it was done only when they had doubts about the department head's competence, and then it was always in the interests of efficiency. When they were alerted about a department that was not doing well, they believed that the best reaction was to tighten controls, "take a closer and more frequent look," and "make sure the department head is on top of things." They quickly added that they did not tell the man in question they were beginning to doubt his competence for fear of upsetting him. Thus, again we see how the values of de-emphasizing the expression of negative feelings and the emphasizing of controls influenced the board's behavior.

The department heads, on the other hand, reported different reactions. "Why are they bothered with details? Don't they trust me? If not, why don't they say so?" Such reactions tended to produce more conformity, antagonism, mistrust, and fear of experimenting. Still another board practice was the "diplomatic"

The department heads, on the other hand, reported different reactions. "Why are they bothered with details? Don't they trust me? If not, why don't they say so?" Such reactions tended to produce more conformity, antagonism, mistrust, and fear of experimenting

Still another board practice was the "diplomatic" rejection of an executive's idea that was, in the eyes of the board, offbeat, a bit too wild, or not in keeping with the corporate mission. The reasons given by the board for not being open about the evaluation again reflected adherence to the pyramidal values. For example, a board member would say, "We do not want to embarrass them," or "If you really tell them, you might restrict creativity."

This practice tended to have precisely the impact that the superiors wished to *avoid*. The subordinates reacted by asking, "Why don't they give me an opportunity to really explain it?" or "What do they mean when they suggest that the 'timing is not right' or 'funds are not currently available'?"

Processes damaged

It is significant that defensive activities like those described are rarely observed during group meetings dealing with minor or relatively routine decisions. These activities become most noticeable when the decision is an important one in terms of dollars or in terms of the impact on the various departments in the organization. *The forces toward ineffectiveness operate most strongly during the important decision-making meetings.* The group and organizational defenses operate most frequently when they can do the most harm to decision-making effectiveness.

Another interesting finding is that the more effective and more committed executives tend to be upset about these facts, whereas the less effective, less committed people tend simply to lament them. They also tend to take on an "I told them so" attitude—one of resignation and noninvolvement in correcting the situation. In short, it is the better executives who are negatively affected.

What Can Be Done?

What can the executive do to change this situation?

I wish that I could answer this question as fully as I should like to. Unfortunately, I cannot. Nevertheless, there are some suggestions I can make.

Blind alleys

First, let me state what I believe will *not* work.

Learning about these problems by listening to lectures, reading about them, or exploring them through cases is not adequate; an article or book can pose some issues and get thinking started, but—in this area, at least—it cannot change behavior. Thus, in one study with 60 top executives:

Lectures were given and cases discussed on this subject for nearly a week. A test at the end of the week showed that the executives rated the lecturers very high, liked the cases, and accepted the diagnoses. Yet when they attempted to apply their newfound knowledge outside the learning situation, most were unable to do so. The major problem was that they had not learned how to make these new ideas come to life in their behavior.

As one executive stated, pointing to his head: "I know up here what I should do, but when it comes to a real meeting, I behave in the same old way. It sure is frustrating." Learning about these problems through a detailed diagnosis of executives' behavior is also not enough. For example:, I studied a top management group for nearly four months through interviews and tape recordings of their decision-making meetings. Eventually, I fed back the analysis. The executives agreed with the diagnosis as well as with the statement by one executive that he found it depressing. Another executive, however, said he now felt that he had a clearer and more coherent picture of some of the causes of their problems, and he was going to change his behavior. I predicted that he would probably find that he would be unable to change his behavior—and even if he did change, his subordinates, peers, and superiors might resist dealing with him in the new way.

The executive asked, "How can you be so sure that we can't change?" I responded that I knew of no case where managers were able to alter successfully their behavior, their group dynamics, and so forth by simply realizing intellectually that such a change was necessary. The key to success was for them to be able to show these new strategies in their behavior. To my knowledge, behavior of this type, groups with these dynamics, and organizational cultures endowed with these characteristics were very difficult to change. What kind of thin-skinned individuals would they be, how brittle would their groups and their organizations be if they could be altered that easily?

Three of the executives decided that they were going to prove the prediction to be incorrect. They took my report and studied it carefully. In one case the executive asked his subordinates to do the same. Then they tried to alter their behavior. According to their own accounts, they were unable to do so. The only changes they reported were (1) a softening of the selling activities, (2) a reduction of their aggressive persuasion, and (3) a genuine increase in their asking for the subordinates' views.

My subsequent observations and interviews uncovered the fact that the first two changes were mistrusted by the subordinates, who had by now adapted to the old behavior of their superiors. They tended to play it carefully and to be guarded. This hesitation aggravated the executives, who felt that their subordinates were not responding to their new behavior with the enthusiasm that they (the superiors) had expected.

However, *the executives did not deal with this issue openly*. They kept working at trying to be rational, patient, and rewarding. The more irritated they became and the more they showed this irritation in their behavior, the more the subordinates felt that the superiors' "new" behavior was a gimmick.

Eventually, the process of influencing subordinates slowed down so much that the senior men returned to their more controlling styles. The irony was that in most cases the top executives interpreted the subordinates' behavior as proof that they needed to be needled and pushed, while the subordinates

interpreted the top managers' behavior as proof that they did not trust their assistants and would never change.

The reason I doubt that these approaches will provide anything but temporary cures is that they do not go far enough. If changes are going to be made in the behavior of an executive, if trust is to be developed, if risk taking is to flourish, he must be placed in a different situation. He should be helped to (a) expose his leadership style so that he and others can take a look at its true impact; (b) deepen his awareness of himself and the dynamics of effective leadership; and (c) strive for these goals under conditions where he is in control of the amount, pace, and depth of learning.

These conditions for learning are difficult to achieve. Ideally, they require the help of a professional consultant. Also, it would be important to get away from the organization—its interruptions, pressures, and daily administrative tensions.

Value of questions

The executive can strive to be aware that he is probably programmed with a set of values which cause him to behave in ways that are not always helpful to others and which his subordinates will not discuss frankly even when they believe he is not being helpful. He can also strive to find time to uncover, through careful questioning, his impact on others. Once in a while a session that is focused on the "How am I doing?" question can enlighten the executive and make his colleagues more flexible in dealing with him.

One simple question I have heard several presidents ask their vice presidents with success is: "Tell me what, if anything, I do that tends to prevent (or help) your being the kind of vice president you wish to be?" These presidents are careful to ask these questions during a time when they seem natural (e.g., performance review sessions), or they work hard ahead of time to create a climate so that such a discussion will not take the subordinate by surprise.

Some presidents feel uncomfortable in raising these questions, and others point out that the vice presidents are also uncomfortable. I can see how both would have such feelings. A chief executive officer may feel that he is showing weakness by asking his subordinates about his impact. The subordinate may or may not feel this way, but he may sense that his chief does, and that is enough to make him uncomfortable.

Yet in two companies I have studied where such questions were asked, superiors and subordinates soon learned that authority which gained strength by a lack of openness was weak and brittle, whereas authority resting on open feedback from below was truly strong and viable.

Working with the qroup

Another step that an executive can take is to vow not to accept group ineffectiveness as part of life. Often I have heard people say, "Groups are no damned good; strong leadership is what is necessary." I agree that many groups are ineffective. I doubt, however, if either of the two leadership patterns described earlier will help the situation. As we have seen, both patterns tend to make the executive group increasingly less effective.

If my data are valid, the search process in executive decision making has become so complicated that group participation is essential. No one man seems to be able to have all the knowledge necessary to make an effective decision. If individual contributions are necessary in group meetings, it is important that a climate be created that does not discourage innovation, risk taking, and honest leveling between managers in their conversations with one another. The value of a group is to maximize individual contributions.

Interestingly, the chief executive officers in these studies are rarely observed making policy decisions in the classic sense, viz., critical selections from several alternatives and determination of future directions to be taken. This does not mean that they shy away from taking responsibility. Quite the contrary. Many report that they enjoy making decisions by themselves. Their big frustration comes from realizing that most of the major decisions they face are extremely complex and require the coordinated, honest inputs of many different executives. They are impatient at the slowness of meetings, the increasingly quantitative nature of the inputs, and, in many cases, their ignorance of what the staff groups did to the decision inputs long before they received them.

The more management deals with complexity by the use of computers and quantitative approaches, the more it will be forced to work with inputs of many different people, and the more important will be the group dynamics of decision-making meetings. If anyone doubts this, let him observe the dry runs subordinates go through to get a presentation ready for the top. He will observe, I believe, that much data are included and excluded by subordinates on the basis of what they believe those at the top can hear.

In short, one of the main tasks of the chief executive is to build and maintain an effective decisionmaking network. I doubt that he has much choice except to spend time in exploring how well his group functions.

Such explorations could occur during the regular workday. For example, In one organization the president began by periodically asking members of his top group, immediately after a decision was made, to think back during the meeting and describe when they felt that the group was not being as effective as they wished. How could these conditions be altered?

As trust and openness increased, the members began to level with each other as to when they were inhibited, irritated, suppressed, confused, and withholding information. The president tried to be as encouraging as he could, and he especially rewarded people who truly leveled. Soon the executives began to think of mechanisms they could build into their group functioning so they would be alerted to these group problems and correct them early. As one man said, "We have not eliminated all our problems, but we are building a competence in our group to deal with them effectively if and when they arise."

Utilizing feedback

Another useful exercise is for the superior and his group members to tape-record a decision-making meeting, especially one which is expected to be difficult. At a later date, the group members can gather and listen to the tape. I believe it is safe to say that simply listening to the tape is an education in itself. If one can draw from skilled company or outside help, then useful analyses can be made of group or individual behavior.

Recently, I experimented with this procedure with an "inside" board of directors of a company. The directors met once a month and listened to tape recordings of their monthly board meetings. With my help they analyzed their behavior, trying to find how they could improve their individual and group effectiveness. Listening to tapes became a very involving experience for them. They spent nearly four hours in the first meeting discussing less than ten minutes of the tape. *'Binds' Created.* One of the major gains of these sessions was that the board members became aware of the "binds" they were creating for each other and of the impact they each had on the group's functioning. Thus:

Executive A was frequently heard antagonizing Executive B by saying something that B perceived as "needling." For example, A might seem to be questioning B's competence. "Look here," he would say, "anyone who can do simple arithmetic should realize that."

Executive B responded by fighting. B's way of fighting back was to utilize his extremely high capacity to verbalize and intellectualize. B's favorite tactic was to show A where he missed five important points and where his logic was faulty.

Executive A became increasingly upset as the "barrage of logic" found its mark. He tended to counteract by (a) remaining silent but manifesting a sense of being flustered and becoming red-faced; and/or (b) insisting that his logic *was* sound even though he did not express it in "highfalutin language" as did B.

Executive B pushed harder (presumably to make A admit he was wrong) by continuing his "barrage of logic" or implying that A could not see his errors because he was upset.

Executive A would respond to this by insisting that he was not upset. "The point you are making is so simple, why, anyone can see it. Why should I be upset?"

Executive B responded by pushing harder and doing more intellectualizing. When Executive A eventually reached his breaking point, he too began to shout and fight.

At this point, Executives C, D, and E could be observed withdrawing until A and B wore each other out.

Progress Achieved. As a result of the meetings, the executives reported in interviews, board members experienced fewer binds, less hostility, less frustration, and more constructive work. One member wondered if the group had lost some of its "zip," but the others disagreed. Here is an excerpt from the transcript of one discussion on this point:

EXECUTIVE A: My feeling is, as I have said, that we have just opened this thing up, and I for one feel that we have benefited a great deal from it. I think I have improved; maybe I am merely reflecting the fact that you [Executive B] have improved. But at least I think there has been improvement in our relationship. I also see signs of not as good a relationship in other places as there might be.

I think on the whole we are much better off today than we were a year ago. I think there is a whole lot less friction today than there was a year ago, but there's still enough of it.

Now we have a much clearer organization setup; if we were to sit down here and name the people, we would probably all name exactly the same people. I don't think there is much question about who should be included and who should not be included; we've got a pretty clean organization.

EXECUTIVE B: You're talking now about asking the consultant about going on with this week's session?

EXECUTIVE A: It would be very nice to have the consultant if he can do it; then we should see how we can do it without him, but it'd be better with him.

EXECUTIVE B: But that's the step, as I understand it, that should be taken at this stage. Is that right?

EXECUTIVE A: Well, I would certainly favor doing something; I don't know what. I'm not making a specific recommendation; I just don't like to let go of it.

EXECUTIVE C: What do you think?

EXECUTIVE D: I'm not as optimistic as A. I wonder if anybody here agrees with me that maybe we haven't made as much progress as we think. I've personally enjoyed these experiences, and I'd like to see them continued.

EXECUTIVE A: Would you like to venture to say why I think we have made progress and why I might be fooled?

EXECUTIVE D: Well, I think maybe you are in the worst position to evaluate progress because if the worst possible thing that can happen is for people to no longer fight and struggle, but to say, "yes, sir," you might call that progress. That might be the worst thing that could happen, and I sort of sense some degree of resignation—I don't think it's progress. I don't know. I might be all alone in this. What do you think?

EXECUTIVE C: On one level it is progress. Whether it is institutional progress and whether it produces commensurate institutional benefits is a debatable question. It may in fact do so. I think it's very clear that there is in our meetings and in individual contact less heat, less overt friction, petulance, tension, than certainly was consistently the case. Do you agree?

EXECUTIVE D: Yes, I think so.

EXECUTIVE C: It has made us a great deal more aware of the extent and nature of the friction and clearly has made all of us intent on fighting less. There's some benefit to it; but there are some drawbacks.

EXECUTIVE A: Well, if you and D are right, I would say for that reason we need more of the program.

Laboratory training

Another possibility is for the executive to attend a program designed to help increase competence in this area, such as laboratory education and its various offshoots ("T-groups," the "managerial grid," "conflict management labs," and so on). These learning experiences are available at various university and National Training Laboratory executive programs. They can also be tailor-made for the individual organization.

I believe outside programs offer the better way of becoming acquainted with this type of learning. Bear in mind, though, that since typically only one or two executives attend from the same organization, the biggest payoff is for the individual. The inside program provides greater possibilities for payoff to the organization.

At the same time, however, it should also be kept in mind that in-house programs *can* be dangerous to the organization. I would recommend that a thorough study be made ahead of time to ascertain whether or not a laboratory educational experience would be helpful to company executives individually and to the organization.

Open discussion

I have never observed a group whose members wanted it to decay. I have never studied a group or an organization that was decaying where there were not some members who were aware that decay was occurring. Accordingly, one key to group and organizational effectiveness is to get this knowledge out into the open and to discuss it thoroughly. The human "motors" of the group and the organization have to be checked periodically, just as does the motor of an automobile. Without proper maintenance, all will fail.

CHAPTER 6
Listening to People

Recently the top executives of a major manufacturing plant in the Chicago area were asked to survey the role that listening plays in their work. Later, an executive seminar on listening was held. Here are three typical comments made by participants:

- "Frankly, I had never thought of listening as an important subject by itself. But now that I am aware of it, I think that perhaps 80% of my work depends on my listening to someone, or on someone else listening to me."

- "I've been thinking back about things that have gone wrong over the past couple of years, and I suddenly realized that many of the troubles have resulted from someone not hearing something, or getting it in a distorted way."

- "It's interesting to me that we have considered so many facets of communication in the company, but have inadvertently overlooked listening. I've about decided that it's the most important link in the company's communications, and it's obviously also the weakest one."

These comments reflect part of an awakening that is taking place in a number of management circles. Business is tied together by its systems of communication. This communication, businessmen are discovering, depends more on the spoken word than it does on the written word; and the effectiveness of the spoken word hinges not so much on how people talk as on how they listen.

The Unused Potential

It can be stated, with practically no qualification, that people in general do not know how to listen. They have ears that hear very well, but seldom have they acquired the necessary aural skills which would allow those ears to be used effectively for what is called *listening*.

For several years we have been testing the ability of people to understand and remember what they hear. At the University of Minnesota we examined the listening ability of several thousand students and of hundreds of business and professional people. In each case the person tested listened to short talks by faculty members and was examined for his grasp of the content.

These extensive tests led us to this general conclusion: immediately after the average person has listened to someone talk, he remembers only about half of what he has heard—no matter how carefully he thought he was listening.

What happens as time passes? Our own testing shows—and it has been substantiated by reports of research at Florida State University and Michigan State University[1]—that two months after listening to a talk, the average listener will remember only about 25% of what was said. In fact, after we have barely learned something, we tend to forget from one-half to one-third of it *within eight hours*; it is startling to realize that frequently we forget more in this first short interval than we do in the next six months.

Gap in Training

Behind this widespread inability to listen lies, in our opinion, a major oversight in our system of classroom instruction. We have focused attention on reading, considering it the primary medium by which we learn, and we have practically forgotten the art of listening. About six years are devoted to formal reading instruction in our school systems. Little emphasis is placed on speaking, and almost no attention has been given to the skill of listening, strange as this may be in view of the fact that so much lecturing is done in college. Listening training—if it could be called training—has often consisted merely of a series of admonitions extending from the first grade through college: "Pay attention!" "Now get this!" "Open your ears!" "Listen!"

Certainly our teachers feel the need for good listening. Why then have so many years passed without educators developing formal methods of teaching students to listen? We have been faced with several false assumptions which have blocked the teaching of listening. For example:

1. We have assumed that listening ability depends largely on intelligence, that "bright" people listen well, and "dull" ones poorly. There is no denying that low intelligence has something to do with inability to listen, but we have greatly exaggerated its importance. A poor listener is not necessarily an unintelligent person. To be good listeners we must apply certain skills that are acquired through either experience or training. If a person has not acquired these listening skills, his ability to understand and retain what he hears will be low. This can happen to people with both high and low levels of intelligence.

2. We have assumed that learning to read will automatically teach one to listen. While some of the skills attained through reading apply to listening, the assumption is far from completely valid. Listening is a different activity from reading and requires different skills. Research has shown that reading and listening skills do not improve at the same rate when only reading is taught.

This means that in our schools, where little attention is paid to the aural element of communication, reading ability is continually upgraded while listening ability, left to falter along on its own, actually degenerates. As a fair reader and a bad listener, the typical student is graduated into a society where the chances are high that he will have to listen about three times as much as he reads.

The barriers to listening training that have been built up by such false assumptions are coming down. Educators are realizing that listening is a skill that can be taught. In Nashville, for example, the public school system has started training in listening from elementary grades through high school. Listening is also taught in the Phoenix school system, in Cincinnati, and throughout the state of North Dakota. About two dozen major universities and colleges in the country now provide courses in listening.

At the University of Minnesota we have been presenting a course in listening to a large segment of the freshman class. Each group of students that has taken listening training has improved at least 25% in ability to understand the spoken word. Some of the groups have improved as much as 40%. We have also given a course in listening for adult education classes made up mostly of business and professional people. These people have made some of the highest gains in listening ability of any that we have seen. During one period, 60 men and women nearly doubled their listening test scores after working together on this skill one night a week for 17 weeks.

Ways to Improvement

Any course or any effort that will lead to listening improvement should do two things:

- Build awareness to factors that affect listening ability.

- Build the kind of aural experience that can produce good listening habits.

At least a start on the first of these two educational elements can be made by readers of this article; a certain degree of awareness is developed by merely discussing factors that affect listening ability. Later we shall discuss some steps that might be taken in order to work at the second element.

Listening to People

Tracks & Sidetracks

In general, people feel that concentration while listening is a greater problem than concentration during any other form of personal communication. Actually, listening concentration *is* more difficult. When we listen, concentration must be achieved despite a factor that is peculiar to aural communication, one of which few people are aware.

Basically, the problem is caused by the fact that we think much faster than we talk. The average rate of speech for most Americans is around 125 words per minute. This rate is slow going for the human brain, which is made up of more than 13 billion cells and operates in such a complicated but efficient manner that it makes the great, modern digital computers seem slow-witted. People who study the brain are not in complete agreement on how it functions when we think, but most psychologists believe that the basic medium of thought is language. Certainly words play a large part in our thinking processes, and the words race through our brains at speeds much higher than 125 words per minute. This means that, when we listen, we ask our brain to receive words at an extremely slow pace compared with its capabilities.

It might seem logical to slow down our thinking when we listen so as to coincide with the 125-wordper-minute speech rate, but slowing down thought processes seems to be a very difficult thing to do. When we listen, therefore, we continue thinking at high speed while the spoken words arrive at low speed. In the act of listening, the differential between thinking and speaking rates means that our brain works with hundreds of words in addition to those that we hear, assembling thoughts other than those spoken to us. To phrase it another way, we can listen and still have some spare time for thinking.

The use, or misuse, of this spare thinking time holds the answer to how well a person can concentrate on the spoken word.

Case of the disenchanted listener. In our studies at the University of Minnesota, we find most people do not use their spare thinking time wisely as they listen. Let us illustrate how this happens by describing a familiar experience:

A, the boss, is talking to B, the subordinate, about a new program that the firm is planning to launch. B is a poor listener. In this instance, he tries to listen well, but he has difficulty concentrating on what A has to say.

A starts talking and B launches into the listening process, grasping every word and phrase that comes into his ears. But right away B finds that, because of A's slow rate of speech, he has time to think of things other than the spoken line of thought. Subconsciously, B decides to sandwich a few thoughts of his own into the aural ones that are arriving so slowly. So B quickly dashes out onto a mental sidetrack and thinks something like this: "Oh, yes, before I leave I want to tell A about the big success of the meeting I called yesterday." Then B comes back to A's spoken line of thought and listens for a few more words.

There is plenty of time for B to do just what he has done, dash away from what he hears and then return quickly, and he continues taking sidetracks to his own private thoughts. Indeed, he can hardly avoid doing this because over the years the process has become a strong aural habit of his.

But, sooner or later, on one of the mental sidetracks, B is almost sure to stay away too long. When he returns, A is moving along ahead of him. At this point it becomes harder for B to understand A, simply because B has missed part of the oral message. The private mental sidetracks become more inviting than ever, and B slides off onto several of them. Slowly he misses more and more of what A has to say.

When A is through talking, it is safe to say that B will have received and understood less than half of what was spoken to him.

Listening to People

Rules for Good Reception

A major task in helping people to listen better is teaching them to use their spare thinking time efficiently as they listen. What does "efficiently" mean? To answer this question, we made an extensive study of people's listening habits, especially trying to discover what happens when people listen well.

We found that good listeners regularly engage in four mental activities, each geared to the oral discourse and taking place concurrently with that oral discourse. All four of these mental activities are neatly coordinated when listening works at its best. They tend to direct a maximum amount of thought to the message being received, leaving a minimum amount of time for mental excursions on sidetracks leading away from the talker's thought. Here are the four processes:

1. The listener thinks ahead of the talker, trying to anticipate what the oral discourse is leading to and what conclusions will be drawn from the words spoken at the moment.

2. The listener weighs the evidence used by the talker to support the points that he makes. "Is this evidence valid?" the listener asks himself. "Is it the complete evidence?"

3. Periodically the listener reviews and mentally summarizes the points of the talk completed thus far.

4. Throughout the talk, the listener "listens between the lines" in search of meaning that is not necessarily put into spoken words. He pays attention to nonverbal communication (facial expressions, gestures, tone of voice) to see if it adds meaning to the spoken words. He asks himself, "Is the talker purposely skirting some area of the subject? Why is he doing so?"

The speed at which we think compared to that at which people talk allows plenty of time to accomplish these four mental tasks when we listen; however, they do require practice before they can become part of the mental agility that makes for good listening. In our training courses we have devised aural exercises designed to give people this practice and thereby build up good habits of aural concentration.

Listening for Ideas

Another factor that affects listening ability concerns the reconstruction of orally communicated thoughts once they have been received by the listener. to illustrate:

The newspapers reported not too long ago that a church was torn down in Europe and shipped stone by stone to America, where it was reassembled in its original form. The moving of the church is analogous to what happens when a person speaks and is understood by a listener. The talker has a thought. To transmit his thought, he takes it apart by putting it into words. The words, sent through the air to the listener, must then be mentally reassembled into the original thought if they are to be thoroughly understood. But most people do not know what to listen for, and so cannot reconstruct the thought.

For some reason many people take great pride in being able to say that above all they try to "get the facts" when they listen. It seems logical enough to do so. If a person gets all the facts, he should certainly understand what is said to him. Therefore, many people try to memorize every single fact that is spoken. With such practice at "getting the facts," the listener, we can safely assume, will develop a serious bad listening habit.

Memorizing facts is, to begin with, a virtual impossibility for most people in the listening situation. As one fact is being memorized, the whole, or part, of the next fact is almost certain to be missed. When he is doing his very best, the listener is likely to catch only a few facts, garble many others, and completely miss the remainder. Even in the case of people who *can* aurally assimilate all the facts that they hear, one at a time as they hear them, listening is still likely to be at a low level; they are concerned with the pieces of what they hear and tend to miss the broad areas of the spoken communication.

When people talk, they want listeners to understand their *ideas*. The facts are useful chiefly for constructing the ideas. Grasping ideas, we have found, is the skill on which the good listener concentrates. He remembers facts only long enough to understand the ideas that are built from them. But then, almost miraculously, grasping an idea will help the listener to remember the supporting facts more effectively than does the person who goes after facts alone. This listening skill is one which definitely can be taught, one in which people can build experience leading toward improved aural communication.

Emotional Filters

In different degrees and in many different ways, listening ability is affected by our emotions.2 Figuratively we reach up and mentally turn off what we do not want to hear. Or, on the other hand, when someone says what we especially want to hear, we open our ears wide, accepting everything—truths, half-truths, or fiction. We might say, then, that our emotions act as aural filters. At times they in effect cause deafness, and at other times they make listening altogether too easy.

If we hear something that opposes our most deeply rooted prejudices, notions, convictions, mores, or complexes, our brains may become overstimulated, and not in a direction that leads to good listening. We mentally plan a rebuttal to what we hear, formulate a question designed to embarrass the talker, or perhaps simply turn to thoughts that support our own feelings on the subject at hand. For example:

The firm's accountant goes to the general manager and says: "I have just heard from the Bureau of Internal Revenue, and. . . ." The general manager suddenly breathes harder as he thinks, "That blasted bureau! Can't they leave me alone? Every year the government milks my profits to a point where. . . ." Red in the face, he whirls and stares out the window. The label "Bureau of Internal Revenue" cuts loose emotions that stop the general manager's listening.

In the meantime, the accountant may go on to say that here is a chance to save $3,000 this year if the general manager will take a few simple steps. The fuming general manager may hear this—if the accountant presses hard enough—but the chances are he will fail to comprehend it.

When emotions make listening too easy, it usually results from hearing something which supports the deeply rooted inner feelings that we hold. When we hear such support, our mental barriers are dropped and everything is welcomed. We ask few questions about what we hear; our critical faculties are put out of commission by our emotions. Thinking drops to a minimum because we are hearing thoughts that we have harbored for years in support of our inner feelings. It is good to hear someone else think those thoughts, so we lazily enjoy the whole experience.

What can we do about these emotional filters? The solution is not easy in practice, although it can be summed up in this simple admonition: *hear the man out*. Following are two pointers that often help in training people to do this:

1. *Withhold evaluation*—This is one of the most important principles of learning, especially learning through the ear. It requires self-control, sometimes more than many of us can muster, but with persistent practice it can be turned into a valuable habit. While listening, the main object is to comprehend each point made by the talker. Judgments and decisions should be reserved until after the talker has finished. At that time, and only then, review his main ideas and assess them.

2. *Hunt for negative evidence*—When we listen, it is human to go on a militant search for evidence which proves us right in what we believe. Seldom do we make a search for evidence to prove ourselves wrong. The latter type of effort is not easy, for

behind its application must lie a generous spirit and real breadth of outlook. However, an important part of listening comprehension is found in the search for negative evidence in what we hear. If we make up our minds to seek out the ideas that might prove us wrong, as well as those that might prove us right, we are less in danger of missing what people have to say.

Benefits in Business

The improvement of listening, or simply an effort to make people aware of how important their listening ability is, can be of great value in today's business. When people in business fail to hear and understand each other, the results can be costly. Such things as numbers, dates, places, and names are especially easy to confuse, but the most straightforward agreements are often subjects of listening errors, too. When these mistakes are compounded, the resulting cost and inefficiency in business communication become serious. Building awareness of the importance of listening among employees can eliminate a large percentage of this type of aural error.

What are some of the specific problems which better listening can help solve?

Less Paper Work

For one thing, it leads to economy of communication. Incidents created by poor listening frequently give businessmen a real fear of oral communication. As a result, they insist that more and more communication should be put into writing. A great deal of communication needs to be on the record, but the pressure to write is often carried too far. The smallest detail becomes "memoed." Paper work piles higher and higher and causes part of the tangle we call red tape. Many times less writing and more speaking would be advisable—*if* we could plan on good listening.

Writing and reading are much slower communication elements than speaking and listening. They require more personnel, more equipment, and more space than do speaking and listening. Often a stenographer and a messenger are needed, to say nothing of dictating machines, typewriters, and other writing materials. Few people ever feel it is safe to throw away a written communication; so filing equipment is needed, along with someone to do the filing.

In oral communication there are more human senses at work than in the visual; and if there is good listening, more can often be communicated in one message. And, perhaps most important of all, there is the give-and-take feature of oral communication. If the listener does not understand a message, he has the opportunity to straighten matters out then and there.

Upward Communication

The skill of listening becomes extremely important when we talk about "upward communication." There are many avenues through which management can send messages downward through a business organization, but there are few avenues for movement of information in the upward direction. Perhaps the most obvious of the upward avenues is the human chain of people talking to people: the man working at the bench talks to his foreman, the foreman to his superintendent, the superintendent to his boss; and, relayed from person to person, the information eventually reaches the top.

- This communication chain has potential, but it seldom works well because it is full of bad listeners. There can be failure for at least three reasons:

- Without good listeners, people do not talk freely and the flow of communication is seldom set in motion.

- If the flow should start, only one bad listener is needed to stop its movement toward the top. M Even if the flow should continue to the top, the messages are likely to be badly distorted along the way.

It would be absurd to assume that these upward communication lines could be made to operate without hitches, but there is no reason to think that they cannot be improved by better listening. But the first steps must be taken by top management people. More and better listening on their part can prime the pumps that start the upward flow of information.

Human Relations

People in all phases of business need to feel free to talk to their superiors and to know they will be met with sympathetic understanding. But too many superiors—although they announce that their doors are always open—fail to listen; and their subordinates, in the face of this failure, do not feel free to say what they want to say. As a result, subordinates withdraw from their superiors more and more. They fail to talk about important problems that should be aired for both parties' benefit. When such problems remain unaired, they often turn into unrealistic monsters that come back to plague the superior who failed to listen.

The remedy for this sort of aural failure—and it should be applied when subordinates feel the need to talk—is what we have called "nondirective listening." The listener hears, really tries to understand, and later shows understanding by taking action if it is required. Above all, during an oral discourse, the listener refrains from firing his own thoughts back at the person talking or from indicating his displeasure or disapproval by his mannerisms or gestures; he speaks up only to ask for clarification of a point.

Since the listener stands the chance of hearing that his most dearly held notions and ideas may be wrong, this is not an easy thing to do. To listen nondirectively without fighting back requires more courage than most of us can muster. But when nondirective listening can be applied, the results are usually worth the effort. The persons talking have a chance to unburden themselves. Equally important, the odds are better that the listener can counsel or act effectively when the time comes to make a move.

Listening is only one phase of human relations, only one aspect of the administrator's job; by itself it will solve no major problems. Yet the past experience of many executives and organizations leaves no doubt, in our opinion, that better listening can lead to a reduction of the human frictions which beset many businesses today.

Listening to Sell

High-pressure salesmanship is rapidly giving way to low-pressure methods in the marketing of industrial and consumer goods. Today's successful salesman is likely to center his attention on the customer-problem approach of selling.

To put this approach to work, the skill of listening becomes an essential tool for the salesman, while his vocal agility becomes less important. *How* a salesman talks turns out to be relatively unimportant because *what* he says, when it is guided by his listening, gives power to the spoken word. In other words, the salesman's listening becomes an on-the-spot form of customer research that can immediately be put to work in formulating any sales talk.

Regardless of the values that listening may hold for people who live by selling, a great many sales organizations seem to hold to the conviction that glibness has magic. Their efforts at improvement are aimed mainly at the talking side of salesmanship. It is our conviction, however, that with the typical salesman the ability to talk will almost take care of itself, but the ability to listen is something in real need of improvement.

In Conference

The most important affairs in business are conducted around conference tables. A great deal has been said and written about how to talk at a conference, how to compromise, how to get problem-centered, and how to cope with certain types of individuals. All these things can be very important, but too frequently the experts forget to say, "First and foremost you must learn to listen at a conference."

Listening to People

The reason for this is simple when we think of the basic purpose for holding almost any conference. People get together to contribute their different viewpoints, knowledge, and experience to members of the group, which then seeks the best of all the conferees' thinking to solve a common problem. If there is far more talking than listening at a conference, however, the oral contributions made to the group are hardly worth the breath required to produce them.

More and better listening at any conference is certain to facilitate the exchange of ideas so important to the success of a meeting. It also offers many other advantages; for example, when participants do a good job of listening, their conference is more likely to remain centered on the problem at hand and less likely to go off on irrelevant tangents.

The first steps toward improved conference listening can be taken by the group leader. If he will simply make an opening statement calling attention to the importance of listening, he is very likely to increase the participants' aural response. And if the leader himself does a good job of listening, he stands the chance of being imitated by the others in his group.

Conclusion

Some businessmen may want to take steps to develop a listening improvement program in their companies. Here are 14 suggestions designed to carry on what we hope this article has already started to do—build awareness of listening.

1. Devote an executive seminar, or seminars, to a discussion of the roles and functions of listening as a business tool.

2. Use the filmed cases now becoming available for management training programs.3 Since these cases present the problem as it would appear in reality, viewers are forced to practice good listening habits in order to be sure of what is going on— and this includes not only hearing the sound track but also watching the facial mannerisms, gestures, and motions of the actors.

3. If possible, bring in qualified speakers and ask them to discuss listening with special reference to how it might apply to business. Such speakers are available at a number of universities where listening is being taught as a part of communication training.

4. Conduct a self-inventory by the employees regarding their listening on the job. Provide everyone with a simple form divided into spaces for each hour of the day. Each space should be further divided to allow the user to keep track of the amount of time spent in reading, writing, speaking, and listening. Discuss the results of these forms after the communication times have been totaled. What percentage of the time do people spend listening? What might improved listening mean in terms of job effectiveness?

5. Give a test in listening ability to people and show them the scores that they make. There is at least one standardized test for this purpose. Discuss the meaning of the scores with the individuals tested.

6. Build up a library of spoken-word records of literature, speeches, and so forth (many can be purchased through record stores), and make them available in a room that has a record player. Also, lend the records to employees who might wish to take them home to enjoy them at their leisure. For such a library, material pertinent to the employees' jobs might be recorded so that those who are interested can listen for educational purposes.

7. Record a number of actual briefing sessions that may be held by plant superintendents or others. When new people go to work for the company, ask them to listen to these sessions as part of their initial training. Check their

comprehension of what they hear by means of brief objective tests. Emphasize that this is being done because listening is important on the new jobs.

8. Set up role-playing situations wherein executives are asked to cope with complaints comparable to those that they might hear from subordinates. Ask observers to comment on how well an executive seems to listen. Do his remarks reflect a good job of listening? Does he keep himself from becoming emotionally involved in what the subordinate says? Does the executive listen in a way which would encourage the subordinate to talk freely?

9. Ask salesmen to divide a notebook into sections, one for each customer. After making a call, a salesman should write down all useful information received aurally from the customer. As the information grows, he should refer to it before each return visit to a customer.

10. Where a sales organization has a number of friendly customers, invite some of the more articulate ones to join salesmen in a group discussion of sales techniques. How do the customers feel about talking and listening on the part of salesmen? Try to get the customers to make listening critiques of salesmen they encounter.

11. In a training session, plan and hold a conference on a selected problem and tape-record it. Afterwards, play back the recording. Discuss it in terms of listening. Do the oral contributions of different participants reflect good listening? If the conference should go off the track, try to analyze the causes in terms of listening.

12. If there is time after a regularly scheduled conference, hold a listening critique. Ask each member to evaluate the listening attention that he received while talking and to report his analysis of his own listening performance.

13. In important management meetings on controversial issues try Irving J. Lee's "Procedure for 'Coercing' Agreement."5 Under the ground rules for this procedure, which Lee outlined in detail in his article, the chairman calls for a period during which proponents of a hotly debated view can state their position without interruption; the opposition is limited to (a) the asking of questions for clarification, (b) requests for information concerning the peculiar characteristics of the proposal being considered; and (c) requests for information as to whether it is possible to check the speaker's assumptions or predictions.

14. Sponsor a series of lectures for employees, their families, and their friends. The lectures might be on any number of interesting topics that have educational value as well as entertainment features. Point out that these lectures are available as part of a listening improvement program.

Not all of these suggestions are applicable to every situation, of course. Each firm will have to adapt them to its own particular needs. The most important thing, however, may not be what happens when a specific suggestion is followed, but rather simply what happens when people become aware of the problem of listening and of what improved aural skills can do for their jobs and their businesses.

CHAPTER 7

A Better Way to Deliver Bad News

Critiquing weak performance is a job nobody likes. But by taking a more open approach, you can be a better boss—and get a lot more from your team. *by Jean-François Manzoni*

Giving feedback to your employees, particularly when their performances fall short of expectations, is one of the most critical roles you play as a manager. For most people, it's also one of the most dreaded. Such conversations can be very unpleasant—emotions can run high, tempers can flare. And so, fearing that an employee will become defensive and that the conversation will only strain the relationship, the boss all too often inadvertently sabotages the meeting by preparing for it in a way that stifles honest discussion. This is an unintentional—indeed, unconscious—habit that's a byproduct of stress and that makes it difficult to deliver corrective feedback effectively.

The good news is that these conversations don't have to be so hard. By changing the mind-set with which you develop and deliver negative feedback, you can greatly increase the odds that the process will be a success—that you will have productive conversations, that you won't damage relationships, and that your employees will make real improvements in performance. In the pages that follow, I'll describe what goes wrong during these meetings and why. I'll look in detail at how real-life conversations have unfolded and what the managers could have done differently to reach more satisfying outcomes. As a first step, let's look at the way bosses prepare feedback—that is, the way they frame issues in their own minds in advance of a discussion.

Framing Feedback

In an ideal world, a subordinate would accept corrective feedback with an open mind. He or she would ask a few clarifying questions, promise to work on the issues discussed, and show signs of improvement over time. But things don't always turn out this way.

Let's consider the following example. Liam, a vice president at a consumer products company, had heard some complaints about a product manager, Jeremy. (Names and other identifying information for the subjects mentioned in this article have been altered.) Jeremy consistently delivered highquality work on time, but several of his subordinates had grumbled about his apparent unwillingness to delegate. They felt their contributions weren't valued and that they didn't have an opportunity to learn and grow. What's more, Liam worried that Jeremy's own career prospects would be limited if his focus on the day-to-day details of his subordinates' work kept him from taking on more strategic projects. As his boss, Liam felt a responsibility to let Jeremy know about his concerns. Here's how the conversation unfolded:

Liam: "I'd like to discuss your work with you. You're doing a great job, and we really value your contributions. But I think you do too much. You have some great people working for you; why not delegate a little more?"

Jeremy: "I don't understand. I delegate when I think it's appropriate. But a lot of people in this company rely on quality work coming out of my department, so I need to stay involved."

Liam: "Yes, and we all appreciate your attention to detail. But your job as a manager is to help your employees grow into new roles and take on more responsibility. Meanwhile, you're so focused on the details that you don't have time to think about the bigger picture, about the direction you're taking this product."

Jeremy: "That's not true. I'm always thinking about the future.

Liam: "I'm just saying, you'd have more time for strategic thinking if you weren't so mired in the day-to-day stuff."

Jeremy: "Are you saying I'm not a strategic thinker?"

Liam: "You're so busy dotting every i and crossing every t that I just don't know what kind of thinking you're capable of!"

This type of exchange is surprisingly common. Each side pushes his point of view more and more aggressively, and the conversation escalates until a relatively minor difference becomes much more dramatic. (For a visual representation of a deteriorating discussion, see the section "Scripted Escalation.") Often, as Liam did in the preceding conversation, one person or the other unintentionally says something overly critical. Of course, it may not get to that point—one or both parties may choose to give in rather than fight. But either way, escalate or fold, the subordinate probably hasn't accepted the news the boss set out to deliver. Managers tend to attribute such nonacceptance to employees' pride or defensiveness. Indeed, it's not unusual for people to feel defensive about their work or, for that matter, to hold inflated views of their performance and capabilities. But more often than not, the boss is also to blame. Let's examine why.

Whenever we face a decision or situation, we frame it, consciously or not. At its simplest, a frame is the decision maker's image of a situation—that is, the way he or she pictures the circumstances and elements surrounding the decision. The frame defines the boundaries and dimensions of the decision or situation—for instance, which issues will be looked at, which components are in and which are out, how various bits of information will be weighed, how the problem might be solved or a successful outcome determined, and so on. Managers tend to frame difficult situations and decisions in a way that is *narrow* (alternatives aren't included or even considered) and *binary* (there are only two possible outcomes—win or lose). Then, during the feedback discussion, their framing remains *frozen*—unchanged, regardless of the direction the conversation takes.

In anticipation of the conversation with Jeremy, for example, Liam framed the problem in his mind as "Jeremy's too controlling." This is a narrow framing because it excludes many alternative explanations—for instance, "Jeremy would really like to hand off some responsibility but doesn't know how and is embarrassed to acknowledge that." Or "Jeremy is actually delegating as much as he can given his subordinates' current skill levels; they are frustrated but really cannot handle more than they do." Or maybe "Jeremy is delegating quite a lot, but Frank and Joan have some other ax to grind." Liam may be making matters worse without realizing it by sending Jeremy mixed signals: "Empower your subordinates, but make no mistakes." We don't know for sure; nor does Liam.

Operating from this narrow view, Liam also approached the discussion with a binary framing that leaves both parties with very little room to maneuver: "Jeremy must learn to delegate or we'll lose Frank and Joan—and meanwhile, he'll burn himself out." Last but not least, Liam's framing remained frozen throughout the exchange despite clear signals that Jeremy was not buying the feedback. At no point was Liam processing, let alone addressing, Jeremy's objections. It's no surprise that the meeting ended badly.

The Dangers of Easing In

After they've had a few bad experiences delivering narrowly framed feedback, managers tend to fall back on the conventional wisdom that it's better to soften bad news with some good.

They try to avoid uncomfortable confrontations by using an indirect approach: They make up their minds about an issue and then try to help their employees reach the same conclusions by asking a carefully designed set of questions.

At first glance, this type of "easing in" seems more open and fair than the forthright approach that Liam took, since the manager is involving the subordinate in a conversation, however scripted. But like the forthright approach, easing in reflects a narrow and binary framing that typically remains frozen throughout the process. Indeed, there would be no need to ease in if the manager were approaching the conversation with a truly open mind. And easing in carries an additional risk: The employee may not give you the answers you're looking for.

For example, Alex, an executive at a pharmaceuticals company, had some difficult news to communicate to one of his subordinates, Erin. She was a middle manager at the company and did an excellent job handling her department but was not contributing satisfactorily to a companywide task force chaired by Alex. Erin was remarkably silent during the meetings, which led Alex to conclude that she was too busy to participate fully and had little to offer the group. Alex's solution? Take her off the task force so she could focus on her primary responsibilities. But because he suspected Erin would be hurt or insulted if he suggested she step down, Alex hoped to prompt her to resign from the committee by asking her a series of questions that would make her see she was too busy to continue. Let's look at what happened.

Alex: "Do you sometimes feel as though you're wasting your time in the task force meetings?"

Erin: "No, I learn a lot from the meetings—and from watching the way you run them."

Alex: "But do you find that your mind is on your daily job when you're at committee meetings?"

Erin: "Not really. I hope I haven't given you the impression that I'm not fully committed. I think this is important work, and I'm excited to be a part of it, and I think I have some good ideas to offer."

Alex: "What if you could participate more informally? You could take yourself off the team as a permanent member, but you could continue to receive the agenda and minutes and contribute when your particular area of expertise is required."

Erin: "It sounds like you want me off the committee. Why? I don't think the committee work has undermined my commitment to my real work. I'm making my numbers. Plus, it's a learning opportunity."

Alex: "No, no, I just want to make sure it's something you really want to do."

Erin: "It is."

As you can see, Erin didn't play along. Alex was not ready for a confrontation, so he folded—and lost. He didn't get Erin off the committee, nor did he communicate his view that her committee work was subpar, so he has no way to help her improve her performance. What's more, he introduced a source of stress into their relationship: Erin is likely to have been unsettled by the interaction, as Alex implied some level of dissatisfaction with her performance without telling her what it is.

As in our previous example, Alex's framing of the issue was narrow: "Erin doesn't talk at the meetings, probably because she's overloaded, so the committee is a waste of her time." His framing was also binary; the interaction could be a success only if Erin agreed to get off the committee without losing her motivation for her regular work. And this framing remained frozen because Alex was concentrating on asking the "right" questions and couldn't process anything but the "right" answers.

Meanwhile, Erin may actually benefit from being on the committee, even if she doesn't say much. She learns a lot, and it gives her visibility. And if she can find a way to contribute more, the committee may well benefit from her membership. But by framing the issue the way he did, Alex excluded other possible solutions, any of which may have been more productive for all concerned: Maybe Erin would talk more in the meetings if Alex probed the reasons for her silence and helped her find a way to contribute what may be very valuable insights. And if overwork is indeed an issue, perhaps there are duties Erin might give up to gain more time and energy.

Easing in is a gamble. You might get lucky, but you have only half the cards. The subordinate may not give you the answers you're looking for, as we saw with Erin, either because she genuinely doesn't agree or because she

sees that the game is rigged and refuses to play along. Or the subordinate may decide to stop resisting and pretend to go along but still fail to believe the feedback. And there's another risk, regardless of how the conversation ends: The employee may forever lose confidence in his or her boss. Erin may always wonder what Alex has up his sleeve, having caught him being disingenuous once.

Indeed, that's what happened to Mark, a marketing director at a large consulting firm. His boss, Rene, had called him into a meeting to discuss his role, and Mark left the meeting having relinquished control of his pet project, developing and implementing the company's first advertising campaign. Rene had asked him a series of seemingly innocuous questions, such as "Do you find endless meetings with different agencies to be a waste of your time?" and "Do you feel like your time would be better spent developing new communications materials?"

Mark eventually accepted what was clearly the "right" conclusion from his boss's perspective—to surrender the project—even though he wanted to continue. Worse, he didn't know why Rene wanted him off the project, so as a learning opportunity, it was wasted. His relationship with his boss is now tainted; Mark can no longer take Rene's comments at face value.

Scripted Escalation

Take a look at how quickly a minor point of difference during a feedback discussion can turn into a major disagreement. Jerry starts the conversation by noting that he'd done a good job on his project. Beth, his boss, is not in violent disagreement with his assessment and acknowledges that "it wasn't bad." Jerry could reaffirm his opening bid but instead tries to pull Beth's view closer to his own by overstating his initial point. Beth disagrees with Jerry's inflated statement, and instead of reiterating her first comment, she yields to the temptation to pull Jerry closer to her point of view. Both present stronger and stronger positions, trying to convince the other, and a minor difference quickly becomes a major point of contention.

Making Feedback More Acceptable

Research shows that people tend to be more willing to accept feedback when they have the feeling that:

- The feedback is reliable and has good intentions toward them.

- The feedback development process is fair—that is, the person giving the feedback collects all relevant information; allows the subordinate to clarify and explain matters; considers the subordinate's opinions; and applies consistent standards when delivering criticism.

- The feedback communication process is fair—that is, the person offering the feedback pays careful attention to the subordinate's ideas; shows respect for the subordinate; and supports the subordinate despite their disagreements.

This short list makes clear the negative impact of approaching a feedback discussion with restrictive framing: Narrow framing tells the employee that the feedback wasn't developed fairly. And a boss constrained by a binary and frozen frame comes across as biased, closed minded, and unsupportive—ensuring that the subordinate will feel as though the feedback hasn't been communicated fairly.

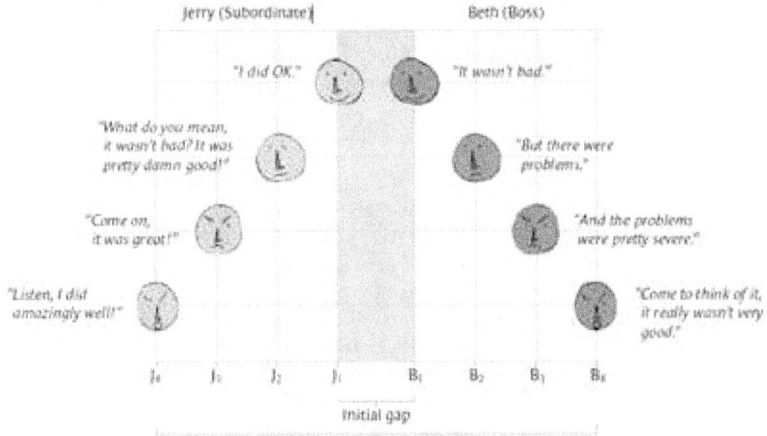

Jerry (Subordinate)   Beth (Boss)

"I did OK."   "It wasn't bad."

"What do you mean, it wasn't bad? It was pretty damn good!"   "But there were problems."

"Come on, it was great!"   "And the problems were pretty severe."

"Listen, I did amazingly well!"   "Come to think of it, it really wasn't very good."

J_4 J_3 J_2 J_1 B_1 B_2 B_3 B_4

Initial gap

Gap at the end of the conversation

Why Is It So Hard?

It's very clear from a distance what went wrong for Liam and Alex. Most managers today are well trained and well meaning; why can't they see what they're doing wrong? The tendency to frame threatening situations in narrow terms can be traced to the combination of several phenomena.

First, research shows that when analyzing others' behavior, most people tend to overestimate the effect of a person's stable characteristics—the individual's disposition and capabilities—and underestimate the impact of the specific conditions under which that person is operating. So, for instance, a manager will attribute a subordinate's performance problems to his or her disposition rather than to circumstances in the workplace, leading to a rather simplistic interpretation. This phenomenon is known as the *fundamental attribution error.*

Second, people are more prone to committing the fundamental attribution error when they operate under demanding conditions. We can better distinguish the impact of situational forces when we have time and energy to spare than when we face multiple demands on our attention. Unfortunately, managers tend to be busy. Facing huge workloads and tight deadlines, they have limited time and attention to engage in exhaustive analyses of all the potential causes of the situations they observe or of the many possible solutions to a given problem. So they settle on the first acceptable explanation. "Jeremy's too controlling" explained all the symptoms, so Liam did not go further.

Research can also give us some insight into why bosses tend to frame things in a binary way. In particular, Harvard Business School professor Chris Argyris's work over nearly five decades has established that under stressful circumstances, people behave in predictable ways. They design their behaviors, often unconsciously, to gain control of a situation and to win—which means, unfortunately, that the other side usually has to lose. That's binary framing.

And why is it so hard for bosses to revise their restrictive framing midstream? For several powerful reasons. First, bosses don't set out to frame situations in restrictive ways; they do so unconsciously, most of the time, and it's hard to question a constraint that we don't know we're imposing on ourselves. Second, humans tend to assume that other reasonable people will see the situation as they see it. That's called the *false consensus effect.* Our framing of an issue represents our view of reality, the facts as we see them. We are reasonable and competent people; why would others see the situation differently?

Bosses can get past these hurdles by recognizing them and becoming more conscious and careful when framing decisions. But then they have to beat another cause of frozen framing: a busy processor. For instance, Liam becomes increasingly stressed as Jeremy continues to push back against his version of the facts, and both devote so much energy to trying to control their growing irritation that they have few resources left to listen, process, and respond constructively.

Reframing Feedback

Let's be clear: I'm not suggesting that bosses systematically misdiagnose the causes of their subordinates' performance problems. Liam's and Alex's early diagnoses may well have been right. And even if their feedback discussions had been more productive, their subordinates may not have been able to sufficiently improve their performances to meet their bosses' expectations. But Jeremy and Erin will almost certainly fail to improve if they don't understand and accept the feedback. Restrictive framing not only makes feedback conversations more stressful than they need to be, it also increases the likelihood that subordinates won't believe what their bosses say. Indeed, subordinates are more likely to accept and act on their bosses' feedback if they feel it is developed and communicated fairly.

So, for instance, imagine how differently Liam and Jeremy's conversation might have gone had the manager framed his concerns more broadly: "I've heard complaints that Jeremy isn't delegating—and some of his employees are feeling sufficiently frustrated that I'm afraid we'll start losing them. I'd like to find out if Jeremy knows about the complaints and get his take on the situation."

This frame isn't narrow. Liam hasn't reached a conclusion about why Jeremy doesn't delegate or whether, indeed, Jeremy is refusing to delegate at all. Nor is the frame binary. Liam hasn't fixed on a win-or-lose outcome. And because Liam hasn't entered the conversation with a preconceived outcome in mind, he has nothing on which to freeze. Now, Liam can open the conversation in a much more open way. He might say, for instance, "Jeremy, I don't know if you're aware of this—or if it's true or not—but I've heard that Frank and Joan are anxious to take on a bit more responsibility. What do you think?" This can lead to a discussion of Frank's and Joan's capabilities, as well as Jeremy's own role and aspirations, without locking Jeremy and Liam into a test of wills.

As for Alex, instead of approaching the meeting with the goal of getting Erin off the committee with minimal damage, he could have framed the interaction more broadly: "I have a great subordinate who doesn't say much on the committee. Let's sit down and talk about her work, the committee, her career plans, and how committee membership fits in with those plans." Because this framing doesn't fix on a win-or-lose outcome, Alex would have felt less need to control the discussion and hence less compelled to ease in.

While most managers can easily see what they're doing wrong when shown how they've developed and presented their feedback, restrictive framing remains a surprisingly persistent problem, even for seasoned managers who excel at other aspects of leadership. But giving feedback doesn't have to be stressful for you, demoralizing for your employees, or damaging to your professional relationships.

Offering more effective critiques requires that you learn to recognize the biases that color the development of feedback. It requires that you take the time to consider alternative explanations for behaviors you've witnessed rather than leaping to hasty conclusions that only serve to paint you and your subordinates into a corner. And it requires that you take into account the circumstances an employee is working under rather than attributing weak performance to the person's disposition.

In short, it requires a broad and flexible approach, one that will convince your employees that the process is fair and that you're ready for an honest conversation.

The Idea in Brief

That dreaded moment has come: You're delivering critical feedback to an employee. Despite your best efforts, the conversation is a disaster: tempers flare, the employee gets defensive, your relationship grows strained.

What happened? Like most managers, you probably inadvertently sabotaged the meeting—preparing for it in a way that stifled honest discussion and prevented you from delivering feedback effectively.

In other words, you most likely engaged in restrictive framing—a *narrow, binary,* and *frozen* approach to feedback: You initiated the conversation without considering alternative explanations for the problem behavior, assumed a win-or-lose outcome, and rigidly maintained your assumptions during the conversation.

Delivering corrective feedback doesn't have to be so difficult—if you use a more open-minded, flexible approach that convinces employees the process is fair.

Restrictive Framing

When preparing to give feedback, you may picture relevant events, decide which information to discuss, and define a solution—all *before* the conversation. This framing sets the stage for trouble.

EXAMPLE: Liam, a VP, hears complaints that Jeremy, a product manager, isn't delegating enough. Liam's framing—"Jeremy's too controlling"—is *narrow* (Liam excludes other possibilities; e.g., Jeremy wants to delegate but doesn't know how) and *binary* (he assumes Jeremy must delegate or his subordinates will leave and he'll burn out). During the conversation, Liam's framing is *frozen* (he neither hears nor addresses Jeremy's objections). Result? Neither Liam nor Jeremy learn from the meeting.

Two Biases

Why do we frame feedback narrowly—despite predictably poor results? Two biases color the feedback process. And the more stressed we are, the more powerful these biases become:

- Fundamental attribution error. We often attribute problems to subordinates' disposition ("Jeremy's too controlling") rather than their circumstances (e.g., perhaps Jeremy *is* delegating, but his subordinates have some other ax to grind). Too busy to identify all potential causes and solutions to a problem, we grab the first acceptable one.

- False consensus effect. We assume others see situations as we do, and fail to revise our framing during feedback sessions.

Reframing Feedback

To avoid the restrictive-feedback trap, watch for these biases. Consider alternative explanations for problems rather than leaping to conclusions.

EXAMPLE: Liam frames his concerns about Jeremy openly: "I've heard complaints that Jeremy isn't delegating—and some of his employees are feeling sufficiently frustrated that I'm afraid we'll start losing them. I'd like to find out if Jeremy knows about the complaints, and get his take."

This framing isn't *narrow* (Liam hasn't leapt to conclusions about the problem's causes) or *binary* (it avoids a win-or-lose outcome). And since Liam avoids a preconceived outcome, he has nothing on which to *freeze*. He initiates the conversation openly: "I don't know if you're aware of this—or if it's true—but I've heard that Frank and Joan are anxious to take on more responsibility. What do you think?"

Why Open Framing Wo rks

Open framing shows you have good intentions, the feedback *development* process was fair (you collected all relevant information), and the *communication* process was fair (you listen to and respect employees).

When employees feel they're getting fair feedback, they accept it more willingly—and work to improve performance.

CHAPTER 8

How to Win the Blame Game

People are often more concerned about avoiding blame than achieving results. But blame can actually be a potent positive force in the workplace. The trick, says this former Major League Baseball pitcher, is knowing how to use it. by David G. Baldwin

When a new product flops in the marketplace or a recent hire turns out to be the employee from hell, blaming somebody for the mistake seems, well, just a tad rude. So people talk politely around the blunder, saying things like "sales targets were missed" or "mistakes occurred," as if the error happened all by itself. Indeed, at many companies, blame is the proverbial elephant in the middle of the room that people pretend isn't there. At other organizations, people are all too quick to point fingers, leaving employees more concerned about avoiding blame than about achieving results. Such organizations, ruled by "CYA," have given blame a bum rap.

The truth is, blame can also be a powerful constructive force. For starters, it can be an effective teaching tool, helping people to avoid repeating their mistakes. When used judiciously – and sparingly – blame can also prod people to put forth their best efforts, while maintaining both their confidence and their focus on goals. Indeed, blame can have a very positive effect when it's used for the right reasons. The key, then, is the way in which blame is managed, which can influence how people make decisions and perform their jobs, and ultimately affect the culture and character of an organization.

Baseball provides an excellent microcosm in which to study blame because mistakes and failures are a routine part of every game. Baseball managers spend most of their time and energy managing things that go wrong. In a typical game, managers, coaches, and players can easily make more than 100 bad decisions – and still end up winning. Even very successful pitchers average more than two bad pitches per batter, and if a player bats .400 (meaning he has succeeded 40% of the time but failed the other 60%), he is having a miraculous season. Thus, if managers, coaches, and owners got upset about every mistake, they would be basket cases by the end of a single game.

I have seen firsthand how blame can affect a baseball organization. During the 1960s and early 1970s, I was a relief pitcher for the Washington Senators (now the Texas Rangers), the Milwaukee Brewers, and the Chicago White Sox. After I left baseball, I continued my educational pursuits in systems engineering and ecological genetics (my undergraduate work was in anthropology and zoology), then worked as a researcher and business consultant. Today I design logic components for processing business data at a San Diego-based company, XMology Corporation.

I recently conducted a study to investigate how managers in Major League Baseball make decisions, and in the course of that survey, I became fascinated by the subject of blame – what functions it serves and how it's best managed. I have come to believe that the way people handle blame plays a major role in shaping an organization's culture. From my observations, both on and off the baseball diamond, I have identified five important rules of blame:

1. Know when to blame – and when not to.
2. Blame in private and praise in public.
3. Realize that the absence of blame can be far worse than its presence.
4. Manage misguided blame.

67

5. Be aware that confidence is the first casualty of blame.

These rules apply to any organization, whether it's the LA Dodgers, General Motors, or a small start-up.

Know When to Blame –and When Not To

In baseball, managers and coaches can correct problems on the field by using blame to assess fault for a mistake – for example, a player missing the signal to steal a base. The goal is to motivate the guilty party to take steps to ensure that he doesn't repeat his error, and the overall result is greater accountability for every player on the team. Used in this positive way, blame benefits all parties: the player, the manager, and the organization as a whole.

Sound simple? Well, it's not. First, many people have little idea when they should – and more important, when they shouldn't – blame someone for a mistake. In baseball, smart managers realize that there are two distinct types of errors: those in which a player failed to execute a physical task properly and those in which he made a decision error (usually called a "mental error" in baseball). An example of the former is a batter who isn't quick enough to catch up with a 98-mph fastball. An instance of the latter is a shortstop who throws to the wrong base because he mistakenly thinks there are two outs instead of one.

Experienced baseball managers realize that coming down hard on a player for a mistake in physical execution usually accomplishes nothing and it could actually harm the player's confidence. But blame can be highly effective in correcting decision errors. Appreciating this difference requires an understanding of how memory works.

Our procedural memory stores information about *how* to do things (the mechanics of throwing a curveball), while our declarative memory stores information about *what* to do (knowing when to throw a curveball to a particular batter). During a game, players must rely on their declarative, not procedural, memory. That is, if a player is aware of the procedure that he's carrying out, then he's in big trouble. Instead, he has to stay focused on the desired result (throwing a fastball knee-high on the outside corner) rather than on how he's doing it (his arm and body position during the throwing motion).When a manager or coach blames a player for an error in physical execution, the player may start to analyze the procedure of what he's doing while he's doing it. This sort of introspection doesn't help during a game; in fact, it can lead to a serious slump. As Yogi Berra once asked,"How can I think and hit at the same time?"

Of course, simple procedural tips can often be effective in reminding players of the basics – "swing through the ball"or "follow through on your throw." Baseball is loaded with aphorisms and rules of thumb to help in this regard. But correcting bad habits or teaching someone a new technique is best done during practice, away from a game situation. A genius at this was Johnny Sain, who was once called the greatest pitching coach who ever lived.

I played briefly for Sain when I was with the White Sox, so I got to observe his technique firsthand. If you had a mechanical (that is, procedural) problem, he would take you off to the side during practice and say, "Why don't you try throwing this way for a few pitches?" And if the new motion was comfortable, he would have you repeat it again and again until you were no longer consciously thinking about what you were doing. In other words, the new technique would become ingrained in your procedural memory. Once you reached that point, he would get you to concentrate on the target again. He had you imagine the ball going to a particular spot – for example, approximately kneehigh on the outside corner – by having the catcher hold his glove there. Soon your mind would be so focused on that goal that you'd be throwing the ball there without even realizing how you were doing it. It's no wonder that Sain, who was a noted pitcher for the Boston Braves and the New York Yankees in the 1940s and 1950s, had a well-earned reputation for his pinpoint control.

Compare Sain's method with the typical approach that managers use for teaching players to make better decisions. Whereas Sain expressed no blame at all, most managers will rebuke a player for decision mistakes, such as ignoring a signal to bunt or choosing to bypass the cutoff man in making a throw to the infield. Blame in such instances does have a positive effect: behavioral scientists have found that reprimands usually evoke a strong emotion in the recipients, which makes them remember the event better so that, when a similar situation arises in the future, they'll make the right decision. To increase this emotional impact, managers will often levy substantial fines. But Sain didn't need to use blame or fines to correct physical-execution errors. He simply reorganized the player's procedural memory.

One category of physical-execution errors, however, deserves a different treatment. A cardinal sin in baseball (actually, in any sport) is a lack of hustle. A classic example is that of an outfielder who misses a fly ball because of his lackadaisical effort. This kind of mistake is considered unforgivable, and managers will often not even bother expending the energy to express blame. In the old days, the player would simply be gone the next day, almost always to a different organization. Contrast this with a player who is making honest physical errors – for example, a batter who has lost his timing. The manager will most likely have him come to the ballpark early for extra batting practice with the hitting coach.

Blame in Private and Praise in Public

As a manager, Ted Williams was always quick to praise his players, and he did so in that larger-than-life manner of his, with great energy and aplomb, which made the recipient feel especially good about what he had done. When Williams criticized a player, he would often do so with the same punctuation that he used for praise, but the dressing-down was always in private, away from the rest of the team and definitely away from outsiders, especially reporters. In fact, I don't recall Williams ever losing his cool and chewing out a player when others were present.

From my own experience, I can tell you that managers and coaches don't have to chastise you in front of everyone to get their points across. As a former pitcher, I felt that I was particularly vulnerable – of all players, pitchers have to make the greatest number of decisions during a game. The catcher signals what kind of pitch to throw, but it's the pitcher who must ultimately make that decision – and bear the responsibility for it. Every pitcher has thrown stupid pitches. Sometimes he'll get away with it, but often the results are disastrous.

I was a sidearm pitcher, but occasionally I would try to surprise a batter by throwing over the top. In a game during 1967, I learned that an overhand curveball was a terrible choice to a righthanded hitter; two years later I learned that it could also be a bad pitch to a lefthanded hitter (that one landed in another time zone). I learned the first lesson from Gil Hodges, the second from Williams. (Hodges, like Williams, was another powerful manager who used the sheer force of his personality to ensure that his praise and blame would not soon be forgotten.) Even after more than 30 years, both lessons, delivered immediately after the game in the privacy of the manager's office, are still fresh in my memory; I will probably carry them to my grave. The point is, Hodges and Williams didn't have to chastise me in front of the whole team to impress upon me the error of my ways. In fact, if they had done that, I might have turned defensive and pigheaded instead of being receptive to their criticism.

Of course, managers are only human, and they can sometimes lose control of their emotions, especially during a tense game. But although lashing out at a player in the dugout might bring some initial relief – letting off steam generally does – the action is usually followed with some regret. Instead, experienced managers have learned to express their anger to someone (or something) else rather than to the player involved. Often, a manager will have a favorite coach who will be close by in the dugout to act as a sounding board, and players learn to maintain a certain distance from the pair.

One of the most egregious violations of the blame-in-private rule occurred in the early 1970s. Ray Kroc had just bought the Padres, and during the opening home game in San Diego, his team wasn't playing as well as he thought it should. So Kroc used the stadium's public-address system to both apologize to the fans and castigate his team. Not surprisingly, players are very sensitive to this sort of thing, and an owner or manager who trashes his team in public quickly gets a bad reputation throughout the league as someone *not* to play for. People like that generally don't last very long in the business. Instead, a savvy manager will tell the media,"Well, we had a tough game and things didn't go our way, but we're going to make a few adjustments." Then he'll meet with his coaches privately to spell out exactly what those adjustments will be.

Realize That the Absence of Blame Can Be Far Worse Than Its Presence

Being criticized by your manager for making a blunder isn't a pleasant experience, but it's much better than no blame at all. When a player screws up and nothing is said, he starts to feel uneasy. "Why didn't someone say something?" he wonders. After all, everyone in the ballpark knows he failed to back up third base on that throw from the outfield. The question in the player's mind is this: "Does the manager care enough to express blame, or does he think I'm hopeless?" If the manager doesn't seem to care, the player's anxiety can build until his imagination begins to run rampant. It can even lead to a touch of paranoia – "They're going to trade me; that explains the silent treatment." So, all in all, it is often much better to express blame because people need to know where they stand. Otherwise, they'll begin to latch onto the worse possible scenario.

I am hardly advocating, though, that a manager freely blame his players every time something goes wrong. As I mentioned earlier, players shouldn't be taken to task for every mistake they make, particularly for errors in physical execution. But this is where scapegoats can play a crucial role. The word "scapegoat" usually carries a negative connotation – somebody unfairly blaming someone else – but the use of scapegoats can frequently be enormously beneficial. In ancient times, Jews would literally pick a goat, upon which they would symbolically place all their sins, and then send the animal out into the wilderness. The process had a healing, cathartic effect –a sense of "closure,"as they say in today's pop psychology lingo – and it allowed blame to be expressed without having to point a finger at the person (or thing) responsible.

Managers and coaches will use anything convenient as a scapegoat. Bad luck and the opposing team are always handy excuses. When an outfielder misses a fly ball, a coach might remark, "Well, the sun was in the wrong spot –those sunglasses won't help you much when that happens." Or when a batter strikes out at a crucial time, the manager might tell one of the coaches to say something to the player; managers rarely talk to players during a game. So a coach might comment,"That last pitch looked like it had great stuff on it,"even though it really didn't. Of course, deep down inside, everyone knows that the pitch was hittable, but the important thing is that the player – who is already well aware how badly he screwed up– is let off the hook, and this helps quiet his fears that he's lost management's confidence and support. Furthermore, the gesture has a larger effect: it reassures the other players that they won't be taken to task for making certain kinds of mistakes. This is why managers will often give undue credit to their opponents, in effect making the other ball club the scapegoat for their own team's woes. (Of course, sometimes the competition really does deserve the credit for simply being better.)

Additionally, a manager might cite questionable calls by the umpires or even try to make himself the scapegoat. Chuck Tanner, who managed the Pittsburgh Pirates to a World Series championship in 1979, was a master at this. If a pitcher had a disastrous sixth inning, Tanner would tell the media, "I should have known he was getting tired." In reality, there might have been no way for Tanner to have known that his man was going to suddenly turn into a battingpractice pitcher, but by taking the heat Tanner made clear his support for that player. Believe me, gestures like that are noticed not only by the player involved but also by everyone else on the team.

Manage Misguided Blame

Of course, sometimes the use of scapegoats can be taken too far, particularly when the player at fault is doing it. In Ring Lardner's classic short story "Alibi Ike," a fictional ballplayer has preformulated excuses ready for any situation. Whatever happens, it isn't his fault. This kind of blame avoidance is a big temptation in baseball. As I mentioned earlier, baseball is an enterprise in which mistakes and failures occur routinely, and those undesirable outcomes can immediately be traced to individuals. In fact, teams hire scorekeepers to do just that. This constant scrutiny makes players feel particularly vulnerable, which can then lead to their making excuses or blaming others for their own mistakes.

I witnessed an extreme case of this on one of my own teams when our center fielder and second baseman went after a lazy pop fly, then both stepped back only to let the ball drop between them. Each blamed the other in the most overt way possible – they began punching each other in the outfield as the live ball lay in the grass a few feet away. This kind of thing rarely happens in the major leagues, but subtler variations do occur. A classic example of blame being redirected to one's teammates is that of a pitcher who blows a game and then, during interviews with the media, blasts his teammates for bad fielding and a lack of offense. A manager might defuse such a potentially damaging situation by redirecting the blame to some scapegoat (perhaps someone wearing a different uniform) before the pitcher has a chance to talk to reporters.

Sometimes, the redirecting of blame is barely perceptible. I remember a first baseman I played with who was somewhat bad at fielding ground balls. To hide this deficiency, he began to "shortarm" balls: he would keep his elbow slightly bent so that he couldn't quite reach difficult grounders. In such instances, official scorekeepers will usually not assign an error on the play because the ball appears to be just out of reach of the fielder. But pitchers are rather sensitive to this kind of thing because every one of the missed balls becomes a hit chalked up against the pitcher. Unfortunately, our coaching staff didn't notice what was happening. (In their defense, people in the dugout can't always see the action on the field very well, and they are usually following the ball anyway and not paying much attention to whether a first baseman's arm is fully stretched out or not.) Of course, the pitchers could have told the coaching staff what was happening, but one unwritten rule is that players don't snitch on their teammates. So the problem persisted,much to the detriment of our team, for more than two years!

Besides detecting and correcting these subtle shifts in blame among players, managers must be acutely aware when they are actually making the situation worse. Players are extremely sensitive to the amounts of blame (and praise) they receive compared to their teammates.Williams,Hodges, and Tanner were well aware that they needed to be careful in this regard, but I've played for managers who seemed to have favorites and were especially hard on other people. This destroyed the trust on the team and led players to second-guess management's decisions. For instance, a player sitting on the bench would begin to wonder whether he really wasn't good enough for the starting lineup (a tough pill to swallow) or whether the manager just had it in for him.

Lastly, a manager should take great pains to correct situations in which others are being blamed for his mistakes. Consider what happened to a pitcher I once played with who had a good arm but who sometimes struggled getting the ball over the plate. He had been in the regular pitching rotation and was doing fine there, but the manager and pitching coach decided that he would be better if he got more rest. So they sat him on the bench for almost three weeks. Well, any pitcher with control problems will only become wilder if he isn't pitching regularly, and for this particular pitcher the experiment was a minor catastrophe. In his next start,he walked the first four or five batters.Then, in desperation, he took some speed off the next pitch to get it into the strike zone and gave up a base hit, prompting the manager to pull him from the game. To outsiders, including the fans present, it looked like the pitcher was a disaster, but those of us in the bull pen knew it wasn't really his fault. We sympathized with him as he returned to the dugout, picked up a bat, and sever

Be Aware That Confidence Is the First Casualty of Blame

Blame can be an effective teaching tool, but overusing it can quickly diminish its effectiveness. At best, repeatedly expressing blame for the same mistakes merely turns into nagging. At worse, too much blame – or the fear of it can completely undermine a person's confidence and seriously damage his ability to perform.

To be successful, pitchers learn that they must concentrate on achieving a positive result ("This pitch is going to be knee-high on the outside corner, and the batter is going to hit an easy grounder to the shortstop") rather than on avoiding a mistake ("This batter is a good high-ball hitter, so I must not give him anything in the upper half of the strike zone").For their part, hitters must focus on seeing the ball as they hit it rather than worry about swinging at a bad pitch or having a pitch called a strike. Otherwise, they'll second-guess themselves, and they won't be able to hit with conviction.

When the fear of blame begins to overtake a team, it starts to erode players'confidence. Soon pitchers are throwing "avoidance" pitches, and batters are being tentative at the plate – and the team is in a slump. At companies, one sure sign that blame has taken over is when employees spend their time building long "Alibi Ike" paper trails (just in case something goes wrong) instead of concentrating on getting results.

Changing that kind of negative environment is not easy. In addition to curtailing the unnecessary blame coursing through the organization (see rules 1 and 4), managers should counteract the damage with a healthy flow of praise. People should be just as likely – if not more so – to be praised for something good they did as to be blamed for something bad. Some managers are naturally generous with their praise – Tommy Lasorda and Frank Lucchesi immediately come to mind–but others feel a little uneasy doing this. Therefore, many managers (the smarter ones anyway) build a coaching staff to complement their personalities. I've played for managers who were aloof, but they hired coaches with cheerleader personalities to keep the praise flowing freely.

Of course, some players can turn even an abundance of blame into a positive force by adopting an "I'll show you" attitude. But people are not usually at their best when they're angry, and most players can handle only so much.blame before it begins to chip away at their confidence. I can't emphasize enough the crucial role that confidence plays in building a winning organization – both confidence in oneself and in one's teammates. I've seen teams that had so-so talent win some close games early in the season, start believing that they can beat anybody, and soon find themselves in a tight pennant race. Experienced managers know this and take great measures to protect their players' confidence. This then makes their jobs particularly tricky – too much blame can erode people's confidence, while too little can hinder them from improving and reaching their full potential.

Achieving that delicate balance is the job of every manager, in business as well as in baseball. Blame can indeed serve some very useful functions within any organization, but it must be managed wisely. The five rules of blame can help managers ensure that they are using it in the most positive and effective ways possible. Otherwise, blame can create problems that are far worse than the unsatisfactory situation that spawned it in the first place.

CHAPTER 9

Leading in Times of Trauma

Once in a great while, tragic circumstances present us with a challenge for which we simply cannot prepare. The terrorist attacks of last September immediately come to mind, but managers and their employees face crises at other times, too. Tragedies can occur at an individual level – an employee is diagnosed with cancer, for example, or loses a family member to an unexpected illness – or on a larger scale – a natural disaster destroys an entire section of a city, leaving hundreds of people dead, injured, or homeless. Such events can cause unspeakable pain not only for the people directly involved but also for those who see misfortune befall colleagues, friends, or even total strangers. That pain spills into the workplace.

The managerial rule books fail us at times like these, when people are searching for meaning and a reason to hope for the future. There is, however, something leaders can do in times of collective pain and confusion. By the very nature of your position, you can help individuals and companies begin to heal by taking actions that demonstrate your own compassion, thereby unleashing a compassionate response throughout the whole organization.

Our research at the University of Michigan and the University of British Columbia's CompassionLab has demonstrated that although the human capacity to show compassion is universal, some organizations suppress it while others create an environment in which compassion is not only expressed but spreads.

Why is organizational compassion important, beyond the obvious and compelling reasons of humanity? Unleashing compassion in the workplace not only lessens the immediate suffering of those directly affected by trauma, it enables them to recover from future setbacks more quickly and effectively, and it increases their attachment to their colleagues and hence to the company itself. For those who witness or participate in acts of compassion, the effect is just as great; people's caring gestures contribute to their own resilience and attachment to the organization. Indeed, we've found that a leader's ability to enable a compassionate response throughout a company directly affects the organization's ability to maintain high performance in difficult times. It fosters a company's capacity to heal, to learn, to adapt, and to excel.

In the following pages, we will describe the actions leaders can take to enable organizational compassion in times of trauma. Before we begin, it's worth noting that some of our examples draw from the events of September 11, 2001, because the magnitude of pain surrounding those events was unprecedented in business history and because the public nature of those events makes the stories relevant to a broad audience. However, pain occurred in the workplace long before last September, and individual and group traumas will continue to disrupt people's daily routines – at times, shattering their lives –as long as humans continue to conduct business.

Beyond Empathy

When people think of compassion, the first thing that comes to mind for many is empathy. But while empathy can be comforting, it does not engender a broader response and therefore has limited capacity for organizational healing. Instead, our research shows that compassionate leadership involves taking some form of public action, however small, that is intended to ease people's pain – and that inspires others to act as well.

TJX president and CEO Edmond English, who lost seven employees aboard one of the planes that hit the World Trade Center, gathered his staff together shortly after the attacks to

her husband's illness and to process its effects on her life. In yet another case, the branch manager at a bank, whose close friend and second-in-command died of a heart attack, took on numerous extra duties and clients so his employees would have additional time to mourn even as he himself was suffering tremendous grief.

This meaning-making process can also be supported by communicating and reinforcing organizational values – reminding people about the larger purpose of their work even as they struggle to make sense of major life issues. When *Newsweek* employees were coping with the unexpected illness and death of editor Maynard Parker, the magazine's editor-in-chief, Richard Smith, at once emphasized the company's commitment to community and its commitment to remaining a world-class newsmagazine. He created an environment in which people could do their best work and at the same time share their sorrow over Parker's losing battle with leukemia. Smith gave daily updates on Parker's condition and stressed that the company was actively involved in getting him top medical care. Knowing that they had ample opportunities to talk about their feelings, and that Parker was getting the best care possible, the *Newsweek* staff could then concentrate on honoring the publication's commitment to remaining a leading newsmagazine – which was particularly meaningful because Parker had so enthusiastically pursued this goal himself. The year's most significant news event was breaking just as Parker fell ill, and *Newsweek* emerged as a leader in the coverage in part because employees wanted to honor Parker in the way he would have valued most–by showing tremendous loyalty in an industry marked by high turnover.

Mark Whitaker, who was then managing editor and succeeded Parker as editor, has reflected on how Smith and others at the top of the organization provided meaning for people that could sustain them through the crisis and beyond. "I think it made people realize, 'Well, if I ever have a situation like that myself, God forbid, this is a company that will be there for me.' That is an intangible thing, but I think it's very powerful," Whitaker recalls. "The way that you deal with tragedy and illness and misfortune in the lives not only of your top people but of all your people really defines your values as an organization."

The Benjamin Group, a Silicon Valley–based public relations firm, demonstrates its values by taking a stand on how employees are treated not only by their colleagues and managers but also by their customers, suppliers, and other business partners.CEO Sheri Benjamin has established a code of principles that includes the statement "We're all in this together," and one implication is that if a client is consistently abusive to firm members, the firm will resign the account.A few years ago, the company dropped a million-dollar account–at that time,worth fully 20% of its annual business. Employees were startled that the firm would go so far, but they were energized, too: Inspired by the knowledge that the PR firm cared about their wellbeing, they worked extra hard to bring in new clients.

A final note on meaning-making: Symbolic gestures can be very powerful.Two days after the September 11 terrorist attacks, England's Queen Elizabeth II asked her troops to play *The Star-Spangled Banner* during the changing of the guard services outside Buckingham Palace. This extraordinary break from a time-honored tradition, dating back to 1660, gave thousands of Americans far from home, as well as supporters from other countries, a way to pay their respects and to mourn.

Actions amid Agony

A context for meaning is the all-important backdrop for creating a compassionate organization, but it is in creating a context for action that leaders can truly unleash an organization's power to heal. As a leader you can set the right example to awaken the potential for compassion, and you can prompt the organizational infrastructure to reinforce and institutionalize compassionate acts.

Perhaps the most important step you can take is to model the behaviors you would like to see others demonstrate. Frequently, people aren't sure if it's appropriate to bring personal matters into the workplace, or they may simply not know how. You can show them, using your status and visibility as a leader.

When a fire destroyed some student living quarters at the University of Michigan Business School, former dean B. Joseph White interrupted his annual "state of the school" speech – typically heavily scripted and highly formal – with some strikingly personal remarks. He assured displaced students that the school would house them and wrote a personal check on the spot to pledge his support. Word of White's actions spread fast, catalyzing a campuswide effort to tap alumni, faculty, and staff networks to find housing, financial support, and other resources for the students affected by the fire.

Leaders can also use their influence to reallocate resources to support people in need. We spoke with the manager of a billing department at one hospital who makes it a point to know the workloads and the personal circumstances of each member of her unit; that way, she can cut people slack when they need extra support. For example, when one employee's husband suffered kidney failure and was awaiting a transplant, the billing manager gave the woman a pager and organized a team of people who could step in and pick up the woman's work on a moment's notice. That way, the employee would be able to take her husband to the hospital without delay if a kidney became available.

In the wake of the September 11 attacks, the MWW Group, a public relations firm based in East Rutherford, New Jersey, juggled its resources so that people could take time off to volunteer at relief organizations. We've also seen leaders redirect funds intended for other purposes to pay for grief counselors in times of collective trauma.

When tragedy strikes, a company's existing infrastructure (its formal and informal networks and routines) can be helpful in locating useful resources, generating ideas, coordinating groups that are not typically connected, and communicating to people what is happening and how the company is responding. For example, after two Macy's stores were badly damaged in the 1994 Northridge, California, earthquake and could not immediately reopen, a store manager used the payroll system to quickly deliver cash to employees whose homes were destroyed. Macy's issued emergency advances of up to $1,000 at a time so that people could secure food, water, and shelter for their families. Following the immediate relief effort, the human resources team used its standard placement routines to search among Macy's stores in Southern California for opportunities to put displaced workers back on the job right away. HR workers quickly determined where help was most needed and then used their networks of employees to establish car pools for people. Within a short time, all employees and undamaged stores were up and running again. People often think of routines as unwieldy processes that interfere with quick response. But in Macy's case, as at other companies we've studied, the established routines helped to expedite matters.

Companies can also set up new routines or networks designed specifically to accelerate aid in the event of a crisis. After a Cisco employee developed a medical emergency while visiting Japan and couldn't find an Englishspeaking health care provider, the company wanted to make sure that no other employee would ever feel so alone in such a frightening circumstance. So it designed a network that would furnish medical assistance to any member of the Cisco family traveling abroad. Interestingly, that network has proved valuable in unexpected ways. In 1998, for instance, civil strife in Indonesia put Jakarta-based employees in the midst of conflict. The company Cisco used to provide international health services sent an ambulance to Cisco's Jakarta headquarters – an ambulance could travel through the streets where no ordinary car could. Employees were loaded into the ambulance, hidden beneath blankets, and driven to a deserted army airstrip where a waiting aircraft took them to safety.

From the Bottom Up

It's essential to note that organizational response doesn't have to start at the top. Leaders need to recognize and support instances where spontaneous organizing and compassionate actions occur at the lower levels of a company. When the organizational context emphasizes and inspires compassionate responses, bottom-up initiatives can take hold and have a transformative effect. Indeed, much of the assistance following the fire at the University of Michigan was generated by staff and students. One student,who did not even know the victims very well, organized more than 40 other students to re-create all the classroom notes from two years of MBA studies and delivered the study materials to the victims within a week of the fire.

At Foote Hospital in Jackson, Michigan, employees wanted to help a colleague who had lost three close rela tives, so they lobbied for a system that would let them donate vacation or personal time to others who needed extra days off. Donating time has now become an official policy at Foote although, of course, contributions are voluntary – thanks to the initiative and innovative thinking of people at the staff level of the organization. This program took on new life in the wake of the attacks in New York and Washington,DC.Foote employees donated more than $18,000 worth of their vacation time to the Red Cross relief fund – again, at their own initiative –and the hospital matched this amount.

At *Newsweek,* one employee organized a blood and platelet donation drive when Maynard Parker fell ill, another managed home chores for Parker's family, and yet another babysat his children. Another bottom-up response arose when Morgan Stanley was devastated by the World Trade Center attacks and had no immediate way to keep track of who was affected. Customer-service representatives from another division of the company took the initiative to organize a vital service: They collected employee information and created a Web site to help the company respond to the needs of individual families.

As these stories show, organizational compassion can be contagious. Indeed, what we call "positive spirals of compassion," where one act of compassion inspires another, are common. At the University of Michigan, for example, MBA students organized a fund-raiser to support victims of the huge earthquake in India last May. When they heard about the relief effort, the leaders of several student clubs contributed the remainder of their club budgets to the drive.

The Case for Compassion

It's hard to document the positive effect that organizational compassion has on employee retention and productivity, but it's clear that employees will reward companies that treat them humanely. On December 11, 1995, a fire destroyed the Malden Mills manufacturing plant in Massachusetts. Instead of taking his $300 million insurance payout and relocating or retiring, owner Aaron Feuerstein decided to rebuild the factory. He announced that he would keep all 3,000 employees on the payroll through December while he started to rebuild. In January, he said he would pay them for a second month, and in February, Feuerstein pledged to pay for a third. His generosity made quite an impact on his employees: Productivity at the plant nearly doubled once it reopened.

Conversely, the costs of not providing leadership and the organizational infrastructure to help people deal with their grief are considerable. People in pain tend to be distracted at work, and if they don't have appropriate outlets, they may become unresponsive and even uncooperative in dealing with colleagues and customers. Just as compassion can be contagious, so can the detachment that accompanies a noncompassionate response; loyalty to the organization erodes not just among people who have directly suffered a tragedy but also among their colleagues who witness the lack of care. Over time, if an organization will not or cannot support the healing process, employee retention will suffer. At one newspaper, a newsroom manager lost his wife to breast cancer. During his wife's extended illness, the employee felt no compassion from his boss; instead he endured complaints about his relatively low level of production. On his first day back to work after the funeral his boss said, "I guess you'll be working those 12-hour days again." The journalist, who was now raising two young children on his own, quit. In another example, a health care employee finally got pregnant after many years of trying, only to deliver a stillborn baby in her eighth month. When the woman's boss stopped by her hospital room, she assumed he was there to offer his condolences. Instead he had come to ask her when she would return to work. Shocked at his lack of compassion, the woman applied to be transferred to another unit, and her manager – who ran a very busy and stretched unit – lost a valued employee with more than ten years of experience.

As a colleague of ours once remarked, there is always grief somewhere in the room. One person may be feeling personal pain due to a death in the family. Another may find personality conflicts in the workplace unbearable. Still another may be watching a colleague struggle with a serious illness and not know how to help. You can't eliminate such suffering, nor can you ask people to check their emotions at the door. But you can use your leadership to begin the healing process. Through your presence you can model behaviors that set the stage for the process of making meaning out of terrible events. And through your actions you can empower people to find their own ways to support one another during painful times. This is a kind of leadership we wish we would never have to use, yet it is vital if we are to nourish the very humanity that can make people – and organizations – great.

Measuring Organizational Compassion

For a quick, high-level check on your organization's capacity for compassion, consider how it performs on the following four dimensions. Each indicator is a measure of the organization's compassion competence, which helps people to heal and continue on with their work when times are bad:

The scope of compassionate response refers to the breadth of resources provided to people in need, such as money, work flexibility, physical aid, and other people's time and attention. If an employee falls ill, is time off the only support, or does the system supply a wide range of healing resources such as variable work hours, gestures of comfort (like food, flowers, and cards), financial support, and assistance with child care?

The scale of compassionate response gauges the volume of resources, time, and attention that people who are suffering receive. Companies that are most effective at unleashing organizational compassion match the scale to the need. When a block of apartments was destroyed in a fire, the people who lived in the apartments, who worked for different companies, found a wide variation in how their companies responded. Some received a routine distribution of insurance coverage. Others were astonished at the outpouring of help from both corporate channels and individual colleagues –money, housewares, furniture, and offers of places to stay. In the latter case, the compassion competence of the system is more likely to help employees heal faster even as it strengthens their loyalty to the company among those who experienced the tragedy directly and among those who witnessed and participated in the response.

Speed of response can vary widely as well. Companies with a competence for compassion extract and direct resources quickly, with little hesitation. Responding compassionately is a hardwired capability. Even in highly regimented bureaucracies, compassion can kick in quickly. In one manufacturing organization, a manager suffered a severe head injury that required almost three months of recovery. This was just after he had been appointed to lead an important experimental project that removed him from the regular compensation scheme and placed him on an incentive pay and benefits system. His previous job had been filled, and he was effectively stuck in no-man's land. A senior operations manager swiftly reinstated the man's previous compensation, obtaining the necessary sign-off without delay, an act that allayed the family's anxiety over its financial circumstances.

Specialization measures the degree to which the system customizes resources to the particular needs of an individual or a group in pain. If, for example, several employees' children are injured in a bus accident, some families will need close communication and hands-on comforting. Others will need to grieve privately and get back to work quickly.

CHAPTER 10

Fear of Feedback

If you're nervous about asking the boss how you're doing, you're not alone Getting the guidance you need requires recognizing your fears, countering them with adaptive techniques, and gathering comments before your annual review. by Jay M. Jackman and Myra H. Strober

No body likes performance reviews. Subordinates are terrified they'll hear nothing but criticism. Bosses, for their part, think their direct reports will respond to even the mildest criticism with stonewalling, anger, or tears. The result? Everyone keeps quiet and says as little as possible. That's unfortunate, because most people need help figuring out how they can improve their performance and advance their careers.

This fear of feedback doesn't come into play just during annual reviews. At least half the executives with whom we've worked *never* ask for feedback. Many expect the worst: heated arguments, impossible demands, or even threats of dismissal. So rather than seek feedback, people avoid the truth and instead continue to try to guess what their bosses think.

Fears and assumptions about feedback often manifest themselves in psychologically maladaptive behaviors such as procrastination, denial, brooding, jealousy, and self-sabotage. But there's hope. Those who learn to adapt to feedback can free themselves from old patterns. They can learn to acknowledge negative emotions, constructively reframe fear and criticism, develop realistic goals, create support systems, and reward themselves for achievements along the way.

We'll look closely at a four-step process for doing just that. But before we turn to that process, let's explore why so many people are afraid to hear how they're doing.

Fear Itself

Obviously, some managers have excellent relationships with their bosses. They receive feedback on a regular basis and act on it in ways that improve their performance as well as their prospects for promotion. Sadly, however, such executives are in the minority. In most companies, feedback typically comes via cursory annual performance reviews, during which managers learn little beyond the amount of a forthcoming raise.

People avoid feedback because they hate being criticized, plain and simple. Psychologists have a lot of theories about why people are so sensitive to hearing about their own imperfections. One is that they associate feedback with the critical comments received in their younger years from parents and teachers. Whatever the cause of our discomfort, most of us have to train ourselves to seek feedback and listen carefully when we hear it. Absent that training, the very threat of critical feedback often leads us to practice destructive, maladaptive behaviors that negatively affect not only our work but the overall health of our organizations. The following are some examples of those behaviors.

Procrastination. We procrastinate –usually consciously – when we feel helpless about a situation and are anxious, embarrassed, or otherwise dissatisfied with it. Procrastination commonly contains an element of hostility or anger.

Consider how Joe, a highly accomplished computer scientist in a large technology company, responded to his frustration over not being promoted. (As with all the examples in this article, people's names have been changed.) Although everyone in the company respected his technical competence, he sensed something was wrong. Instead of seriously assessing his performance and asking for feedback, he became preoccupied with inessential details of his projects, played computer solitaire, and consistently failed to meet project deadlines. When

81

Joe asked about his chances for advancement in his annual review, his boss singled out Joe's repeated failure to finish projects on time or to seek formal extensions when he knew work would be late. In fact, Joe's continued procrastination became a serious performance issue that cost him a promotion.

Denial. We're in denial when we're unable or unwilling to face reality or fail

to acknowledge the implications of our situations. Denial is most often an unconscious response.

Angela, a midlevel manager in a consulting firm, drifted into a state of denial when a hoped-for promotion never materialized. Her superiors told her that she hadn't performed as well as they'd expected. Specifically, they told her she'd requested too much time off to spend with her children, she hadn't sufficiently researched a certain industry, she hadn't met her yearly quota of bringing in ten new clients, and so on. Every time she tried to correct these problems, her male superiors put her off with a new series of excuses and challenges. The fact was, they had no intention of promoting her because they were deeply sexist. Accepting that fact would have required Angela to leave, but she chose instead to live in denial. Rather than recognize she was at a dead end, she did nothing about her situation and remained miserable in her job.

Brooding. Brooding is a powerful emotional response, taking the form of morbid preoccupation and a sense of foreboding.Faced with situations they feel they can't master, brooders lapse into passivity, paralysis, and isolation.

Adrian, a training manager, brooded when his boss set forth several stretch goals for him. Believing the goals to be unrealistic, Adrian concluded that he couldn't meet them. Rather than talk with his boss about this, he became desperately unhappy and withdrew from his colleagues. They in turn saw his withdrawal as a snub and began to ignore him. The more they avoided him, the more he brooded. By the end of six months, Adrian's brooding created a self-fulfilling prophecy; because he had met none of his goals, his new projects were assigned to someone else, and his job was in jeopardy.

Jealousy. Comparing ourselves with others is a normal behavior, but it becomes maladaptive when it is based on suspicion, rivalry, envy, or possessiveness. Jealous people may overidealize others whom they perceive to be more talented, competent, and intelligent; in so doing, they debilitate themselves.

Leslie, a talented vice president of a public relations firm, fell into the jealousy trap when her boss noted during a meeting that one of her colleagues had prepared a truly excellent report for a client. Leslie began comparing herself with her colleague, listening carefully to the boss's remarks during meetings and noting his smiles and nods as he spoke. Feeling that she could never rise to her colleague's level, Leslie lost all enthusiasm for her work. Instead of seeking a reality check with her boss, she allowed the green-eyed monster to consume her; ultimately, she quit her job.

Self-Sabotage. Examples of self-sabotage, usually an unconscious behavior, are all too common.Even national leaders such as Bill Clinton and Trent Lott have hoisted themselves on their own petards.

Workplaces are full of people who unconsciously undercut themselves. Take, for example, the story of Nancy, a young associate who found herself unable to deal with more than two projects at once. During her review, Nancy resented her boss's feedback that she needed to improve her ability to multitask. But instead of initiating further discussion with him about the remark, she "accidentally"made a nasty comment about him one day within his earshot.As a result, he began looking for ways to get rid of her. When she was eventually fired, her innermost feelings of unworthiness were validated.

These and other maladaptive behaviors are part of a vicious cycle we have seen at play in too many organizations. Indeed, it's not uncommon for employees, faced with negative feedback, to rain private maledictions upon their supervisors. No wonder, then, that supervisors are reluctant to give feedback. But when employees'imagined and real fears go unchecked, the work environment becomes dysfunctional, if not downright poisonous.

Learning to Adapt

Adapting to feedback – which inevitably asks people to change, sometimes significantly – is critical for managers who find themselves in jobs, companies, and industries undergoing frequent transitions. Of course, adaptation is easier said than done, for resistance to change is endemic in human beings. But while most people feel they can't control the negative emotions that are aroused by change, this is not the case. It is possible and necessary – to think positively about change. Using the following adaptive techniques, you can alter how you respond to feedback and to the changes it demands.

Recognize your emotions and responses. Understanding that you are experiencing fear ("I'm afraid my boss will fire me") and that you are exhibiting a maladaptive response to that fear ("I'll just stay out of his way and keep my mouth shut") are the critical initial steps toward adaptive change. They require ruthless self-honesty and a little detective work, both of which will go a long way toward helping you undo years of disguising your feelings. It's important to understand, too, that a particular maladaptive behavior does not necessarily tell you what emotion underlies it: You may be procrastinating out of anger, frustration, sadness, or other feelings. But persevering in the detective work is important, for the payoff is high. Having named the emotion and response, you can then act – just as someone who fears flying chooses to board a plane anyway.With practice, it gradually becomes easier to respond differently, even though the fear, anger, or sadness may remain.

Maria,a midlevel manager with whom we worked, is a good example of someone who learned to name her emotions and act despite them. Maria was several months overdue on performance reviews for the three people who reported to her. When we suggested that she was procrastinating, we asked her how she felt when she thought about doing the reviews. After some reflection, she said she was extremely resentful that her boss had not yet completed her own performance evaluation; she recognized that her procrastination was an expression of her anger toward him. We helped her realize that she could act despite her anger. Accordingly, Maria completed the performance evaluations for her subordinates and, in so doing, felt as if a huge weight had been lifted from her shoulders. Once she had completed the reviews, she noticed that her relationships with her three subordinates quickly improved, and her boss responded by finishing Maria's performance review.

We should note that Maria's procrastination was not an entrenched habit, so it was relatively easy to fix.Employees who start procrastinating in response to negative emotions early in their work lives won't change that habit quickly –but they can eventually.

Get support. Identifying your emotions is sometimes difficult, and feedback that requires change can leave you feeling inhibited and ashamed. For these reasons, it's critical to ask for help from trusted friends who will listen, encourage, and offer suggestions.Asking for support is often hard, because most corporate cultures expect managers to be self-reliant. Nevertheless, it's nearly impossible to make significant change without such encouragement. Support can come in many forms, but it should begin with at least two people – including, say, a spouse, a minister or spiritual counselor, a former mentor, an old high school classmate – with whom you feel emotionally safe. Ideally, one of these people should have some business experience. It may also help to enlist the assistance of an outside consultant or executive coach.

Reframe the feedback. Another adaptive technique, reframing, allows you to reconstruct the feedback process to your advantage. Specifically, this involves putting the prospect of asking for or reacting to feedback in a positive light so that negative emotions and responses lose their grip.

Take the example of Gary, a junior sales manager for a large manufacturing company. Gary's boss told him that he wasn't sociable enough with customers and prospects. The criticism stung, and Gary could have responded with denial or brooding. Indeed, his first response was to interpret the feedback as shallow. Eventually, though, Gary was able to reframe what he'd heard, first by grudgingly acknowledging it. ("He's right, I'm not very sociable. I tested as an introvert on the Myers-Briggs, and I've always been uncomfortable with small talk.") Then Gary reframed the feedback. Instead of seeing it as painful, he recognized that he could use it to help his career. Avoiding possible maladaptive responses, he was able to ask himself several important questions: "How critical is sociability to my position? How much do I want to keep this job? How much am I willing to change to become more sociable?" In responding, Gary realized two things: that sociability was indeed critical to success in sales and that he wasn't willing to learn to be more sociable. He requested a transfer and moved to a new position where he became much more successful.

Break up the task. Yet another adaptive technique is to divide up the large task of dealing with feedback into manageable, measurable chunks, and set realistic time frames for each one. Al though more than two areas of behavior may need to be modified, it's our experience that most people can't change more than one or two at a time. Taking small steps and meeting discrete goals reduces your chances of being overwhelmed and makes change much more likely.

Jane, for example, received feedback indicating that the quality of her work was excellent but that her public presentations were boring. A quiet and reserved person, Jane could have felt overwhelmed by what she perceived as the subtext of this criticism: that she was a lousy public speaker and that she'd better transform herself from a wallflower into a writer and actress. Instead, she adapted by breaking down the challenge of "interesting presentations"into its constituent parts (solid and wellconstructed content; a commanding delivery; an understanding of the audience; and so on). Then she undertook to teach herself to present more effectively by observing several effective speakers and taking an introductory course in public speaking.

It was important for Jane to start with the easiest task – in this case, observing good speakers. She noted their gestures, the organization of their speeches, their intonation, timing, use of humor, and so forth. Once she felt she understood what good speaking entailed, she was ready to take the introductory speaking course. These endeavors allowed her to improve her presentations. Though she didn't transform herself into a mesmerizing orator, she did learn to command the attention and respect of an audience.

Use incentives. Pat yourself on the back as you make adaptive changes. That may seem like unusual advice, given that feedback situations can rouse us to self-punishment and few of us are in the habit of congratulating ourselves. Nevertheless, nowhere is it written that the feedback process must be a wholly negative experience. Just as a salary raise or a bonus provides incentive to improve performance, rewarding yourself whenever you take an important step in the process will help you to persevere in your efforts. The incentive should be commensurate with the achievement. For example, an appropriate reward for completing a self-assessment might be an uninterrupted afternoon watching ESPN or, for a meeting with the boss, a fine dinner out.

Getting the Feedback You Need

Once you've begun to adapt your responses and behavior, it's time to start seeking regular feedback from your boss rather than wait for the annual performance review to come around. The proactive feedback process we recommend consists of four manageable steps: self-assessment, external feedback, absorbing the feedback, and taking action toward change. The story of Bob, a vice president of human resources, illustrates how one executive used the four-step process to take charge of his work life.

When we first met Bob, he had been on the job for three years and felt he was in a feedback vacuum. Once a year, toward the end of December, Harry – the gruff, evasive CEO to whom he reported– would call Bob in, tell him what a fine job he had been doing, announce his salary for the following year, and give him a small bonus. But this year, Bob had been dealing with thorny issues – including complaints from senior female executives about unfair compensation – and needed some real feedback. Bob wondered how Harry viewed his work. Were there aspects of Bob's performance that Harry wasn't happy with? Did Harry intend to retain Bob in his current position?

Self-Assessment. We encouraged Bob to begin by assessing his own performance. Self-assessment can be a tough assignment, particularly if one has never received useful feedback to begin with. The first task in self-assessment was for Bob to determine which elements of his job were most important. The second was to recall informal feedback he had received from coworkers, subordinates, and customers – not only words, but facial expressions, body language, and silences.

Bob took several weeks to do his selfassessment. Once we helped him realize that he was procrastinating with the assessment, he enlisted a support system – his wife and an old college buddy – who encouraged him to finish his tally of recollections. At the end of the process, he recognized that he had received a good deal of positive informal feedback from many of the people with whom he interacted. But he also realized that he was too eager to please and needed to be more assertive in expressing his opinions. We helped him reframe these uncomfortable insights so that he could see them as areas for potential growth.

External Feedback. The next phase of the proactive process–asking for feedback – is generally a two-part task: The first involves speaking to a few trusted colleagues to collect information that supports or revises your self-assessment. The second involves directly asking your boss for feedback. Gathering feedback from trusted colleagues shouldn't be confused with 360-degree feedback, which culls a wide variety of perspectives, including those from people who may not know you well. By speaking confidentially with people you genuinely trust, you can keep some of the fear associated with feedback at bay. Trusted colleagues can also help you identify your own emotional and possibly maladaptive responses to criticism, which is particularly beneficial prior to your meeting with your superior. Additionally, feedback conversations with colleagues can often serve as a form of dress rehearsal for the real thing. Sometimes, colleagues point out areas that warrant immediate attention; when they do, it's wise to make those changes before meeting with the boss. On the other hand, if you think you can't trust any of your colleagues, you should bypass such feedback conversations and move directly to setting up a meeting with your boss.

Bob asked for feedback from two trusted colleagues, Sheila and Paul, at meetings that he specifically scheduled for this purpose. He requested both positive and negative feedback and specific examples of areas in which he did well and in which he needed to improve. He listened intently to their comments, interrupting only for clarification. Both told him that he analyzed problems carefully and interacted well with employees. Yet Sheila noted that at particularly busy times of the year, Bob seemed to have difficulty setting his priorities, and Paul pointed out that Bob needed to be more assertive. Armed with his colleagues' feedback, Bob had a clearer notion of his strengths and weaknesses. He realized that some of his difficulties in setting priorities were owing to unclear direction from Harry, and he made a note to raise the matter with him.

The next step in external feedback –the actual meeting with your boss requires delicate handling, particularly since the request may come as a surprise to him or her. In setting up the meeting, it's important to assure your boss that criticisms and suggestions will be heard, appreciated, and positively acted on. It's vital, too, to set the agenda for the meeting, letting your superior know that you have three or four questions based on your self-assessment and feedback from others. During the meeting, ask for specific examples and suggestions for change while remaining physically and emotionally neutral about the feedback you hear. Watch carefully not only for specific content but also for body language and tone, since feedback can be indirect as well as direct. When the meeting concludes, thank your boss and indicate that you will get back to her with a plan of action after you've had time to absorb what you've heard. Remember, too, that you can terminate the meeting if it becomes counterproductive (for example, if your boss responds to any of your questions with anger).

During his feedback meeting with Harry, Bob inquired about his work priorities. Harry told him that the company's financial situation looked precarious and that Bob should focus on locating and implementing a less costly health benefit plan. Harry warned Bob that a new plan would surely anger some employees, and because of that, Bob needed to develop a tougher skin to withstand the inevitable criticisms.

As Bob learned, feedback meetings can provide more than just a performance assessment; they can also offer some other important and unexpected insights. Bob had been so immersed in HR issues that he had never noted that Harry had been otherwise preoccupied with the company's financial problems.

Absorbing the Feedback. Upon hearing critical feedback, you may well experience the negative emotions and maladaptive responses we described earlier. It's important to keep your reactions private until you can replace them with adaptive responses that lead to an appropriate plan of action.

Bob, for example, realized he felt irritated and vaguely hurt at the suggestion that he needed to toughen up. He brooded for a while but then reframed these feelings by recognizing that the negative feedback was as much a commentary on Harry's preoccupations as it was on Bob's performance. Bob didn't use the reframing to negate Harry's feedback; he accepted that he needed to be more assertive and hard-nosed in dealing with employees' issues.

Taking Action. The last phase of the proactive feedback process involves coming to conclusions about, and acting on, the information you've received. Bob, for example, chose to focus on two action strategies: implementing a less costly health care plan – which included preparing himself to tolerate employee complaints – and quietly looking for new employment, since he now understood that the company's future was uncertain. Both of these decisions made Bob uncomfortable, for they evoked his fear of change. But having developed his adaptive responses, he no longer felt trapped by fear. In the months following, he implemented the new health benefits plan without taking his employees' criticisms personally. He also kept an eye on the company's financials and reconnected with his professional network in case it became clear the organization was starting to founder.

The Rewards of Adaptation

Organizations profit when executives seek feedback and are able to deal well with criticism. As executives begin to ask how they are doing relative to management's priorities, their work becomes better aligned with organizational goals. Moreover, as an increasing number of executives in an organization learn to ask for feedback, they begin to transform a feedback-averse environment into a more honest and open one, in turn improving performance throughout the organization.

Equally important, using the adaptive techniques we've mentioned can have a positive effect on executives' private lives. When they free themselves from knee-jerk behaviors in response to emotions, they often find that relationships with family and friends improve. Indeed, they sometimes discover that rather than fear feedback, they look forward to leveraging it.

Reframe Your Thinking

Almost everyone dreads performance reviews, which typically take place once a year. But how you respond to the boss's feedback – and how often you request it – will largely affect your performance and chances for career advancement. We've found that getting beyond that sense of dread involves recognizing and naming the emotions and behaviors that are preventing you from initiating feedback discussions. Once you determine those emotional and behavioral barriers, it's a matter of reframing your thoughts and moving toward more adaptive behavior. Below are some examples of how you might turn negative emotions into more positive, productive thoughts.

Possible Negative Emotion	Maladaptive Response	Reframing Statement
Anger *(I'm mad at my boss because he won't talk to me directly.)*	Acting out *(stomping around, complaining, being irritable, yelling.*	It's up to me to get the feedback I need.
Anxiety *(I don't know what will happen.)*	Brooding *(withdrawal, nail biting)* Avoiding *(I'm too busy to ask for feedback.)*	Finding out can open up new opportunities for me.
Fear of confrontation *(I don't want to do this.)*	Denial, rocrastination, self-sabotage *(canceling meetings with boss)*	Taking the initiative puts me in charge and gives me some power.
Fear of reprisal *(If I speak up, will I get a pink slip?)*	Denial *(I don't need any feedback. I'm doing just fine.)*	I really need to know honestly how I'm doing.
Hurt *(Why did he say I wasn't trying hard enough?)*	Irritability, jealousy of others *(silence, plotting to get even)*	I can still pay attention to what he said even though I feel hurt.
Defensiveness *(I'm better than she says.)*	Acting out by not supporting the boss *(You can bet I'm not going to her stupid meeting.)*	Being defensive keeps me from hearing what she has to say.
Sadness *(I thought he liked me!)*	Brooding, withdrawal *(being quieter than usual, feeling demotivated)*	How I'm doing in my job isn't about whether I'm liked.
Fear of change *(How will I ever do all that he wants me to do?)*	Denial *(keep doing things the same way as before)*	I *must* change to keep my job. I need to run the marathon one mile at a time.
Ambivalence *(Should I stay or should I go?)*	Procrastination, passivity *(waiting for somebody else to solve the problem)*	What really serves my interests best? Nobody is as interested in my well-being as I am. *I* need to take some action now.
Resignation *(I have to leave!)*	Resistance to change *(It's just too hard to look for another job. It's not really so bad here.)*	I'll be much happier working somewhere else.